THE URBAN
KALEIDOSCOPE
CANADIAN PERSPECTIVES

McGraw-Hill Ryerson Series in Canadian Sociology

General Editor - Lorne Tepperman

A STATISTICAL PROFILE OF CANADIAN SOCIETY,
Daniel Kubat and David Thornton

IDEOLOGICAL PERSPECTIVE ON CANADA, 2nd Edition,
M. Patricia Marchak

SOCIAL MOBILITY IN CANADA,
Lorne Tepperman

CANADIAN SOCIETY IN HISTORICAL PERSPECTIVE,
S.D. Clark

CRIME CONTROL: THE URGE TOWARD AUTHORITY,
Lorne Tepperman

THE DISREPUTABLE PLEASURES: CRIME AND DEVIANCE IN CANADA,
John Hagan

UNDERSTANDING DATA,
B.H. Erickson and T.A. Nosanchuk

THE MAKING OF THE CANADIAN MEDIA,
Paul Rutherford

SOCIAL PSYCHOLOGY AS POLITICAL ECONOMY,
W.P. Archibald

THE NEW URBAN POOR,
S.D. Clark

SOCIOLOGICAL THEORIES OF EDUCATION,
Raymond Murphy with the collaboration of Ann Denis

DEMOGRAPHIC BASES OF CANADIAN SOCIETY, 2nd Edition
Warren Kalbach and Wayne McVey

FRAGILE FEDERATION: SOCIAL CHANGE IN CANADA,
Lorna Marsden and Edward Harvey

THE CANADIAN CLASS STRUCTURE, 2nd Edition,
Dennis Forcese

THE SURVIVAL OF ETHNIC GROUPS,
Jeffrey G. Reitz

WOMEN, FAMILY AND THE ECONOMY,
Sue Wilson

THE URBAN KALEIDOSCOPE: CANADIAN PERSPECTIVES,
Leslie W. Kennedy

Forthcoming

RELIGION: CONSENSUS, CONFLICT AND CHANGE,
Roger O'Toole

THE URBAN KALEIDOSCOPE
CANADIAN PERSPECTIVES

Leslie W. Kennedy
Department of Sociology
University of Alberta
Edmonton, Alberta

McGraw-Hill Ryerson Limited
Toronto   Montreal   New York   St Louis   San Francisco   Auckland
Bogotá   Guatemala   Hamburg   Johannesburg   Lisbon
London   Madrid   Mexico   New Delhi   Panama   Paris   San Juan
São Paulo   Singapore   Sydney   Tokyo

The Urban Kaleidoscope: Canadian Perspectives

1 2 3 4 5 6 7 8 9 0   D   2 1 0 9 8 7 6 5 4 3

Printed and bound in Canada by John Deyell Company

Canadian Cataloguing in Publication Data

Kennedy, Leslie W., date
The urban kaleidoscope

(McGraw-Hill Ryerson series in Canadian sociology)
Includes index.
ISBN   0-07-548561-3

1. Sociology, Urban.   2. Urbanization - Canada.
3. City and town life - Canada.   I. Title.   II. Series.

HT 127.K46   307.7'6'0971   C83-098321-X

C.2

39,005

To my parents

To Ilona, LLL

Contents

Editor's Introduction

Some books are so intellectually tidy as to deaden the reader with pre-digested theories and endless problems neatly solved. This is not one such book. When you finish reading it, urban sociology seems bigger and more complex than it did when you started. That is what I find most exciting about *The Urban Kaleidoscope: Canadian Perspectives.*

Urban sociology has always seemed like a miniature version of sociology as a whole. Many of the most interesting problems get fought out in urban sociology and, accordingly, they get fought out in the pages of this short, fast moving book. The relationship between social and natural environments, where sociology borders on demography, ecology and geography, is one such problem area. Another is the interaction between formal and informal social structures, and the evolution of such structures as communities, neighbourhoods, social networks and the like. Some interesting debates about inter-group dynamics — for example, segregation, prejudice, conflict, and cooperation — are held in the literature on cities; as are important discussions about normative integration, anomie and social pathology, crime and social control, cognition, socialization, and the formation of tastes.

Historically, cities were seed-beds of new rights, "citizenship rights," as Max Weber, T.H. Marshall and Henri Pirenne have shown us. Thus, urban sociology is a field for studying the development of social choice, middle class individualism, and deviant lifestyles. But cities are also mini-states, within which classes and interest groups clash to gain control over often vast resources — sometimes over matters of principle and sometimes not. Professor Kennedy touches on these themes too and brings us up to date on the conditions of various Canadian cities today. Thus the book can be read both as a discussion of theories of city life and of life in Canada's main cities in the late twentieth century.

Our cities are changing in many ways that are difficult to understand. There is no longer a simple one way flow from countryside to small city to large city, for example, or from central core to suburb. Accordingly, the author spends some time discussing the current policy and planning questions in urban and community development, and the kinds of politics associated with them. He is at home with the conflict perspective as a way of thinking about city structure and change. But Professor Kennedy is also at home with the application of empirical research to policy and political debate, and spends some time discussing the way evaluation research and social impact assessment are being used in this debate.

New communication and transportation technology may very well revolutionize Canadian cities within our lifetime. Communities need no longer be primarily locational, or based on proximity, and it follows that anything that increases our communication reach increases both our effective community size and our simultaneous access to multiple communities. Does this mean even more decentralization of city living, a new kind of city, or perhaps even the demise of cities as we have known them for 500 years? Forecasting the likely change depends on a good understanding of everything Professor Kennedy has told us, and more besides. Readers who enjoy thinking of questions, as well as thinking of answers, will feel exhilarated by this book, which is, I am sure, exactly what the author intended.

Lorne Tepperman

Preface

Over the years that I have been teaching urban sociology I have always been amazed by how many examples I can use from daily newspapers. Urban studies is a living thing. But for many years we have suffered in this country from course material that does not relate to our own experience in Canadian cities. We have had to piece together the daily newspaper reports with books that have been written for other audiences in other nations.

It is my hope that this book will help to offset this problem. I have tried to apply universal theories to the Canadian context to show the student of cities how we fit into the world context and how our cities grow and develop. I have also tried to present my ideas with an eye to the importance of applying them in social planning. Cities are so much a part of our lives that their complexity can confuse us, can create conflict, and can destroy our quality of life. Knowing how cities work and how people adapt to them will provide us with the tools to cope with problems in future cities, making them better places in which to live.

Acknowledgements

If you are like me, this is one of the first things that you read when you pick up a new book. A book is a product of many people speaking through one author and the acknowledgements page gives the author a chance to name and thank some of those people, however inadequately.

I believe that one should salute one's roots. My early training in urban studies was inspired by William Michelson, at the University of Toronto. The Centre for Urban and Community Studies was a friendly home to me for two years.

The attraction of this area of sociology was further reinforced on coming to the University of Alberta. Earle Snider has been a friend and advisor. He has shown me how to take ideas and make them real and I thank him for that most of all. Dennis Stokes, my companion in work, helped me test ideas and took time out from a busy schedule to read the final draft. His assistance is greatly appreciated. Ron Gillis provided a number of insights, as well as encouragement. Harvey Krahn provided helpful criticisms on an early draft at a time when his graduate school commitments were the greatest. Joan Blishen, of McGraw-Hill Ryerson, encouraged me to write the book and made it possible for me to publish it.

To the staff in the Population Research Laboratory — Ilze Hobin, Tana Hilbrecht, Cliff Kinzel, Kerri Calvert, Lynette Hussain, and Dr. Lalu — goes my gratitude as well. I have plagued them with many requests, while ignoring many of theirs, during the writing of this book.

Finally, I would like to thank my wife, Ilona, for her support and encouragement. She has spent many hours reading and commenting on the manuscript, and thus improving it.

THE URBAN KALEIDOSCOPE
CANADIAN PERSPECTIVES

1 The Urban Kaleidoscope: Common Factors and Unique Features

A. INTRODUCTION TO URBAN CONCEPTS

Impressions of Cities as Places to Live

The popular view of cities is a negative one. Despite the fact that so many people live there, it is commonly believed that cities are cold, anonymous and unfriendly. It is said that cities are places of strangers. The breakdown of family ties and the loss of a sense of community are seen as products of urban living.

White and White (1962) have argued that this "anti-urbanism" has been most vociferous from intellectuals who have dealt with city life in their writings and professional work. In their review of the major American thinkers (including philosophers, politicians, architects, and sociologists), White and White found great hostility towards city life. Thoreau (1969), who extolled the traditional values of rural living from his retreat by Walden Pond, set the example for those who saw a need to escape the negative aspects of urban life. This retreat from the city became popular again in the late nineteen-sixties. The idealized life was that removed from urban congestion and tension.

The anti-urbanism theme is found in Canadian literature, as well. In *Surfacing*, Margaret Atwood presents a view of cities as confusing and alienating (Atwood, 1972). The true escape from their deadening influence is the rural landscape. Hugh Garner's descriptions of Cabbagetown in Toronto contain similar views of the life of the poor in an inner city (Garner, 1978). In *Duddy Kravitz*, the main character is driven to own land outside of the city of Montreal in a back-to-the-country retreat from city values (Richler, 1969).

The focus of much of this literature rests on what Banfield (1974) identifies as problems coming from the unfulfilled promises of urban life. When expectations are high and resources are limited,

1

conflict can emerge between groups. The struggle for limited amenities within cities leads to tension between groups differing in income, education, and ethnic backgrounds. Some groups fail to compete as well as others and get less; this inevitably leads to further inter-group conflict. This tension, combined with anonymity, is said to lead to alienation and social breakdown, with problems of divorce, family disputes, mental illness, and crime all believed to be consequences.

The belief that cities are always anonymous places to live is now being challenged by researchers who have found strong friendship and kin ties among urban residents. These ties are maintained despite contact with a large number of strangers on a daily basis. Selective interaction takes place and adjustment to contact with strangers is a normal part of city life. These findings indicate a need to move beyond particularistic, impressionistic images of the city to more comprehensive accounting of city processes and change.

We can study the city in a way that allows us to understand more completely the urban phenomenon. This involves a number of tasks. First, we need to systematically compare the population of one city to that of another, using important socio-demographic criteria. Second, the behaviour of individuals and the social psychological factors that govern this behaviour must be studied. Third, we need to isolate important processes that contribute to structural changes in the city. Fourth, we must identify the relationship between behaviour and the physical structure of the city. Fifth, we must offer ways of resolving problems of a lack of congruence between individual adaptation (behaviourally and attitudinally) to the physical, economic, and political structure of the city.

These steps allow us to understand how cities differ from one another. As well, they indicate to us the commonalities of the urban experience from one city to the next. As a general introduction to the study of cities, we can examine each of these steps.

We can be guided in this overview by Cohen's review of urban problems (Cohen, 1973). He outlines a number of factors that contribute significantly to the problems of large industrial cities. Some of these problems relate to scale and expanse. Some are primarily political. Some are managerial and administrative. Others are sociological and cultural in character. All relate to what Cohen has referred to as the problem of "disgovernance" in industrial cities. Disgovernance reflects a concern about difficulties encountered in identifying problem areas found in cities and making decisions to solve these problems (Cohen, 1973:454). The outline of these problems will provide a quick review of issues to be dealt with in detail in the following chapters of this book.

Problems in Cities versus Urban Problems

When we address urban issues from the point of view of social analysis, should we be studying the city as a specific problem area? Alternatively, should we worry about such things as crime or housing separately? Crime is an urban problem but is it a problem created by urbanism? Should we study crime separately from factors, such as urban alienation, that may contribute to certain types of criminal behaviour? Understanding the nature of the city and identifying urban processes is a way of coming to grips with particular social concerns.

How do we select the important differences in cities? How do we isolate common features that all cities share? Where do we start in our attempt to break down, into manageable terms, the complexity of the city? Cities differ because their governments have varying ideas about what services and facilities are required. Cities can vary according to the type of people who live there. They may also have different types of industry as employers of these people. But if they contrast in all these ways, how can we ever hope to understand the ways in which cities, in general, function? Can we learn anything from our experiences in one city to help us in studying another?

One factor we can use to compare cities is size. The size of the metropolis provides the basis for specialization. It allows for economies and efficiencies difficult to obtain in smaller units. However, it also leads to the need for rigid standards and administration to handle this complexity. The loss of individual control and mastery over the environment is considered an important negative consequence of the problem of size.

In a few years, there will be cities containing 20 to 30 million people. The problems of inadequate water supply, energy, transportation facilities, park space, and housing are concentrated in small areas. Pollution, traffic congestion, and overcrowding in housing have called for strategies to draw people away from the large cities. By imposing green belts around the metropolitan boundaries or by building new towns a distance away, planners hope to relieve congestion. The big cities keep getting bigger, however, and pose serious dilemmas for governments trying to contain urban sprawl.

The increased size of cities not only creates internal problems but also has spillover effects on the surrounding countryside. The desire for single-family housing, for example, led to a strong suburban movement in North American cities in the 1950s and 1960s. The consequences for urban life and the changes that had to be made to the urban structure to accommodate this move were monumental. These involved changing transportation patterns with the building of highways and rapid transit systems. There were losses of economic trade from inner cities to suburban shopping centres. Unhappiness and alienation emerged in suburban environments, leading to a call for better social services and recreational facilities.

In addition to size, population concentration and the mixing of differing social groups present problems for accommodation to city life. Often new arrivals to cities are confronted with difficulties with language or cultural differences. Cities have, in turn, had to accommodate to these newly arrived minorities. There have been major political struggles to readjust the ways in which services and resources are allocated to meet the needs of these groups.

Competition for space and resources develops among people of different backgrounds in cities. This is further aggravated by high levels of population density in the confined spaces of urban areas. Further problems arise in cities experiencing the effects of large concentrations of certain demographic groups, for example, young people. Mexico City and many large metropolises in Latin America, where close to half of the population is less than 15 years of age, must attempt to provide shelter and employment opportunities at unprecedented levels.

North American and European cities, meanwhile, are also faced with different but related problems. As these societies age, there are increasingly older populations to service. In London, there are one million people over the age of 65. Providing shelter, transportation, and social services to this group constitutes a massive commitment of city resources. The problems of demographic change require a basic understanding of the ways populations change and their geographical distribution. The difficulties encountered by special groups, such as the elderly and the young, require attention in our study of urban issues.

The Bases for Urban Lifestyles

The term "urbanism" refers to the ways of living in cities. Michelson (1975) has argued that urban life styles constitute the most important factors in defining urban life. Life styles contrast according to the nature of one's background. More importantly, they are a function of expectations about how one wants to live. The choice to remain child-free, for example, leads to different types of expectations about housing and recreational activities than does the choice to have children. The life styles that evolve from choice or from groups that have no choice, such as the poor, make demands on the urban structure.

Further, the highly intertwined nature of urban living has led to problems when the system is broken at any point. This becomes evident when service personnel, such as bus drivers or policemen, decide to strike for more pay. Traditional systems of voicing concerns — meetings, conferences, and public hearings — lose their impact. An escalation of demands, an immoderation of expression, and a disruption of daily life become the norm.

The city, among other things, is a competitive arena where people struggle for improved opportunity, status, and recognition. In bigger cities, competition is heightened. The stakes and rewards are higher. The gaps between groups widen and those left behind become more disenchanted and more difficult to service (Cohen, 1973).

The traditions promoted by religion or political groups are important for urban studies, as well. When these values change conflict develops between groups who feel that their values should be recognized. For example, there has been a debate for years in Canada about keeping stores open on Sunday (the "blue" laws are statutes which fine businesses that open on Sunday). This debate derives from a conflict between those who argue that traditionally the "day of rest" is a time for families. People should not be required to go to work. On the other side are those who find that Sunday is a good time for them to shop. Work commitments and other activities make this difficult at other times during the week. Also, the fact that many small stores and entertainment facilities are allowed to stay open on Sundays further confuses the issue.

Governments have generally tried to stay out of the conflict and maintain the status quo. The problem is that, recently, large stores have begun to challenge the laws. The government is being forced to take action through the courts, thereby bringing the conflict out in the open. Changes in values demand action when conflicts emerge. Any changes in the laws will inevitably lead to drastic changes in the retail business in cities. The resolution of these and related conflicts for the benefit of all people living in cities challenges the imagination of urban policymakers and researchers.

Structural Changes in the Metropolis

The problems of urban sprawl, pollution, and the distribution of tax burdens also create problems in cities. Inner cities suffer double jeopardy. They may receive no suburban tax support, yet must face the highest concentration of social problems.

The "urban reform" movements in North America have forced many suburban areas to combine with inner-city governments to share the costs of maintaining urban services, many of which are extensively used by suburban commuters. In Canada, the metropolitan (two-tier) government system is a response to the structural problems of inner cities faced with expensive services but limited revenues. Metropolitan Toronto, Ottawa-Carleton, Hamilton-Wentworth, Metropolitan Montreal, Metropolitan Vancouver, and others are examples of two-tier systems. These structures allow for certain autonomy at the local level for physical planning and the delivery of social services. Transportation, police, fire and transit costs are shared at the metropolitan level. The problems of inequities in revenues and costs in administering cities are not completely solved by these structures. The overwhelming problems of inner cities often demand a disproportionate amount of resources in police, fire, and other emergency services at the expense of outlying areas. The reapportioning of these services is complicated and challenges the allocation rules of urban administrators.

While there are strong benefits for city living which derive from the implementation of important city services, they have tended to be difficult to review and change. The functionaries who manage and operate the city system may develop a stake in the "system" and, over time, they may consider changes that benefit their job performance rather than meeting the demands of the consumers.

The overriding influence of the bureaucracy has led to a lack of intermediary representation through elected officials. Mayors' offices are generally understaffed and are subject to a constant crossfire of different interests in the city looking for solutions to problems. The vulnerability of mayors to this pressure weakens their ability to run the city.

The development of the role of "gatekeeper" has also made the politicians' work more difficult. Gatekeepers may run bureaucracies in a way that is not responsive to political pressure. This has led to an increase in concerns about open government in cities. The need for responsive government has been discussed by advocates of citizen participation. They argue that, in many cities, decisions about services and resources are not made or influenced by the people most directly affected by the decisions, i.e. the consumers of the services. In Canadian cities the debate about management of resources has evolved from discussions about political changes (ward reviews, citizen action groups); policy changes in setting goals; and structural changes in increasing government accountability.

The increasing size of the city and the growth of large service systems have contributed to the alienation of the receivers of services from the systems that serve them. The massive growth of the public sector to deliver services not available or affordable from the private sector has led to disincentives for the renderer of services. With the increasing importance of the public sector in providing services has come an increasing expectation that people will obtain the services that they need and want. This has become increasingly difficult with the growing cost of delivery and the growing resistance to tax increases.

The trend in Canadian cities, faced with large debts to pay for services, is to cut back or to privatize. What is still unclear is how much cutback can be absorbed in a system before its effectiveness disappears. For example, how many policemen can be laid off before the streets are unacceptably unsafe? Recent experiences with police strikes in Halifax and Montreal indicate that without a police presence, delinquent acts occur at an unprecedented degree. Can we provide adequate levels of protection through the use of private (and sometimes cheaper) protection services? Who suffers from the cutbacks? These are issues to be addressed in this book.

Social versus Physical Structures in Cities

It is stating the obvious to point out that cities without people do not exist. It is surprising to note, however, that many of the people who study cities treat them as though they are simply physical settings with buildings and roads. It has been popular to attribute animal- or human-like character to cities, as well. Recently, the mayor of Mexico City described its problems as being those of an old man. ". . . (its) digestion and respiration are difficult, drainage is a problem, circulation is bad." (*Newsweek,* July 12, 1982:53). Cities are often talked about as living organisms. If the functions of the city are impaired in any way we talk about decay or urban malaise. What an analogy to make about a conglomeration of people and buildings! Yet isn't it the way we look at a city — as if it were able to take on its own character?

Following this logic, it is easy to argue that by producing good physical environments the problems faced in cities, such as crime, ethnic tension, and poverty, disappear. This "deterministic" view of the city has led to a wide variety of planning strategies. These have attempted to resolve urban problems without considering their consequences on people's lives and the quality of the social environments in which they live. Social processes contribute to the ways in which cities develop and change. It is vital to understand these processes in order to make plans for resolving urban social problems. Individual choice affects housing markets. Demand for political involvement influences government decision-making. The desire for clean and safe environments to raise children encourages the move to the suburbs. The hope for crime-free neighbourhoods puts heavy demands on police resources. The expectation of employment attracts people to cities. These are some of a long list of issues that can only be addressed through the development of conceptual schemes for analyzing basic social processes and the ways in which they are accommodated in the physical setting of the city.

An example of this conflict between physical and social solutions is found in the urban renewal projects developed in North America in the 1960s and 1970s. Renewing older areas within the inner cities without disrupting viable communities has posed serious difficulties. The decay and decline in these areas has proved to be reversible. However, many of the tactics used in displacing current residents without any attention being paid to the preservation of the community have led to serious conflicts in the implementation of these programmes. The difficulties in tenant relocation and the increased militancy of neighbourhood groups have made urban renewal all but impossible. On the other hand, the community consultative process, essential as it may be, nevertheless causes lengthy delays in the processing of public projects from conception to construction. These delays lead to significant increases in the costs of construction.

A sense of community in neighbourhoods is difficult to maintain in the face of development pressure and threats from transportation corridors cutting areas in half. The value of community has led to arguments which extol the virtues of rehabilitating rather than rebuilding neighbourhoods. The investment of human and economic capital in the revitalization of inner-city areas has been a major step in cutting the slide towards decay. It also helps make these areas safer and better-quality environments.

B. URBAN PROBLEM-SOLVERS: THE ROLE OF SOCIOLOGY

Urban problems derive from the size, density, and heterogeneity of cities; their structural characteristics; the conflict of urban life styles; the problems of "disgovernance"; and the congruence between social and physical structures. The mandate of research is to define the nature of social problems and their antecedents. In a study of a representative sample of Canadian urban sociologists, Van Vliet (1979) found that while there was little agreement among researchers about what constituted the major urban stressors in Canada, they do agree that sociologists have a role in the problem-solving process. Respondents in the study were asked to rank the three greatest urban problems. Poverty shows up as the most frequently mentioned primary urban stressor. Transport and social isolation are also seen as primary concerns. Other areas which create stress include housing and racial or ethnic discrimination (Van Vliet, 1979:12).

The problems of the poor are the problems of urban living but the poor feel these problems most acutely. They have the most difficulty competing for scarce resources in the city and finding suitable housing in locations close to work. They have the most problems dealing with social control agencies, such as the police, and have the greatest need for social services. The poor also tend to suffer from ethnic or racial discrimination. This discrimination and lack of resources can combine to alienate the poor from family and friends and snare them in a web of unfulfilled expectations.

While the poor are the ones who suffer most from urban problems, the concerns of housing, crime, and discrimination also affect other income groups. The importance of recognizing the negative results of endemic social breakdown in cities occurring in these areas has led sociologists to apply their research to practical problem-solving.

Pioneer work on urban problem-solving in the United States was done in Chicago in the early 1920s by the human ecologists led by Robert Ezra Park. Park was a journalist who came to the University of Chicago at a time when rapid changes were taking place in that metropolis. There was a massive immigration of new Americans from all over the world. It was evident to anyone living in Chicago at the time that large-scale problems of housing, transportation, crime, and ethnic and racial tension were building. Park and his associates set out to examine these problems and offer insights into the ways in which they could be solved. In Chapter 4, we will be discussing the theories that developed in the school of human ecology which emerged from this work.

Of greatest importance in reviewing the Chicago school is acknowledging their belief that research on social problems could be joined with active problem-solving. This work could include steps to provide adequate social services (provided in Chicago in the form of settlement houses, an idea which still prevails today in many Canadian cities); proper shelter; recognition of ethnic and racial tension and its geographic structure; and initial ideas about the role of physical planning in providing ways of changing the structure of cities to help alleviate major areas of social problems.

Ideas about the ways in which these issues should be approached have evolved since Park's time. Urban settlements have changed. With these changes, there have been alterations in the view that society has of cities as viable places to live. This has led to the emergence of successive schools of thought in urban sociology, each of which has focussed on different variables to improve the explanatory power of current theories.

Van Vliet (1979) demonstrates, in his research, that Canadian urban sociologists have adopted a variety of strategies for approaching urban problem-solving. There is a widespread belief that research can provide important insights into urban policymaking. Just as we said that the researcher must pose questions to begin an examination of urban processes, these questions are often asked in the urgency of trying to solve specific problems. Variations in life styles can lead to conflict among groups over the definitions of social problems. For example, the growing acceptability of the use of soft drugs does not dissuade those who argue that this is a first step towards the use of more deadly substances. The counter-argument is that making cannabis use illegal creates problems for law enforcement. It also criminalizes people who are otherwise law-abiding. The contrast in perspectives and in beliefs makes defining the problem in this area very difficult. The recommendations for problem-solving are also going to vary according to one's perspective.

In sum, a research agenda will reflect the ways in which the problem is defined, the bias of the researcher, the immediacy of the problem for policy, and the findings of other researchers doing work in this area. The urban research agenda covers the broad spectrum of the human experience in cities. Now, how does this translate into operational terms?

C. FORMULATING URBAN PERSPECTIVES: AN OUTLINE

Urban Concepts and Hypotheses Testing

We first need a framework of analysis to study urban problems. When we examine cities in systematic terms, we enter into a more abstract evaluation of social processes. How, for example, does a large increase of immigrants affect the social life within inner-city neighbourhoods? Are there differences in living conditions in cities that are large compared to those that are small? Does high-density living lead to juvenile delinquency or psychological stress? These questions are examples of testable hypotheses — questions that need answers.

The ways in which we attempt to answer these questions are often affected by our view of what we consider to be the important factors contributing to patterns of living in cities. For example, as we pointed out earlier, some researchers believed that by improving the physical environment of the city we could make the living conditions for its inhabitants much better. Removing slum areas would remove social problems. This point of view identified specific physical factors as having an important effect on the social structure of the city. For example, decaying homes can lead to problems in family relations. This, in turn, leads to crime. By removing these areas and replacing them with new housing we would then be able to reduce crime. Research on this problem has been done. The hypotheses that were tested identified the relationship between important physical and social variables, as pointed out above. Once these relationships are established, further studies can be done to test the initial findings. It is then a short step to generalize these findings to all cities.

We may feel uncomfortable with the perspective that physical improvements in cities lead to social improvements (which in the case of the physical determinists led to such policies as urban renewal). The research task then involves finding the flaws in this approach by offering a better explanation. In evaluating the direct cause-effect relationship between the physical environment and social behaviour, some researchers argued that this approach ignored the importance of intervening variables, such as age, sex or income. For example, low-income people who were moved to new environments were not any happier than when they lived in the slums. In fact, they were very disgruntled. Where they had friends and neighbours that they could rely on in the old neighbourhood, these friends simply were too far away from the new home. They could no longer be relied upon for mutual support on a day-to-day basis. Creating better physical environments, in other words, may be a negative step if social concerns are not considered.

The requirement in urban research is for approaches that delineate common patterns of social life in cities and that isolate factors affecting these patterns. What emerges is a theoretical perspective. This should offer a conceptual framework which outlines how research should proceed. We acknowledge the unique features of cities. It is their commonalities, however, that provide the bases for research and planning.

The Urban Kaleidoscope

We can understand the ways in which theory and social events are distinguished through the analogy of the kaleidoscope. The pieces of the kaleidoscope (i.e. the glass and the cylinder) are the same from one time to another. The mechanisms for bringing the pieces together in certain patterns (e.g. gravity, the roundness of the cylinder) operate all the time. The characteristics of the glass (e.g. colour, value) look the same from one turn to another. The patterns that are formed, however, change with different combinations of the shards of glass.

So it is with the way in which variables in the city combine to create unique forms. The processes and the characteristics of the variables which contribute to the character of cities can be isolated through the theoretical formulation of urban research. It is the task of the researcher to identify the processes at work in cities. A theory must then be formulated that provides concepts defining these processes, and outlines the ways in which these concepts are related. Ethnicity, age, income, and sex provide the hue and shape to urban populations. How these factors combine is a matter for research. Seeing how the light strikes the glass and the gravity forms the shapes in the kaleidoscope gives actual ideas about the basis for change of the pictures formed in the cylinder. Migration, fertility, ethnic tension, and city growth give us a basis for analyzing the factors that contribute to urban patterns.

The evolution of perspectives in approaches to urban research and problem-solving is summarized by Sjoberg (1970). He identifies eight distinct perspectives that have been used in urban sociology.

These theories range from an explanation of the reasons for the initial development of cities to outlining the importance of political power in the configuration of urban settlements. What these perspectives share is a belief that the major variables used in each theory best explain urban change. The theories in urban sociology have generally emphasized the variables that explain the "source" of change. While we will use this outline as a guide, our emphasis will rest on describing the "process" of change. So, while urban researchers have talked about the bases for community power in terms of the types of social institutions that develop, we will be concerned, as well, with the way in which these institutions allocate the resources that they have available. This "process-oriented" approach provides us with a way of accounting for important factors in urban research while still capturing the aspects of urban change.

Sjoberg states that the overriding purpose of urban sociology is to understand and predict the nature of change in the social and ecological structure of the city (Sjoberg, 1970:86). He classifies the major schools of thought in urban sociology based on the variable or variables to which each gives priority. The list includes the technological, environmental, subsocial, ecological complex, economic, urbanization, value-orientation, and social power schools. We can briefly look at each of these.

Technology and the Origins of Cities

Technological innovation is a major cause of change in urban settlement patterns. The population movement from preindustrial to industrial cities accompanied changes in social order brought about by technological innovation. The movement away from societies relying on hunting and gathering for sustenance to ones that developed surpluses through the planting and harvesting of grain led to dramatic changes. These changes affected settlement patterns. The advent of inanimate energy sources (e.g. steam and electricity) in agriculture and manufacturing in the industrial era has had equally dramatic effects on societies. The industrial cities that have grown up are products of this technological change. This approach is the specific emphasis of researchers such as Sjoberg (1960).

Technological success in agriculture and industry is often a function of environment. Environment (e.g. climate and geography) is a major factor linked to the origins of cities. For example, the restrictions on urban development that arise as a result of inadequate water resources or the shortage of land can have serious consequences for urban growth.

The current debate over the environmental problems encountered with pollution are also addressed in this perspective, especially in the cases where these problems are aggravated by the original site chosen for a city. For example, the serious smog problems in Los Angeles are greatly magnified by the fact that the air pollution is trapped in the bowl created by the mountains surrounding the city. We will include technology and environment in a discussion of the origin of cities.

Urban Transformation

The focus of the urbanization school relates to the patterns and processes involved in the transition from preindustrial or feudal ways of life to an industrial/urban/capitalistic order. This perspective is best typified by the work of Louis Wirth (1938) in his study of "urbanism as a way of life" and by Robert Redfield (1953) in his study of the folk-urban continuum. To Wirth (1938:10) the city is best characterized by changes in size, density, and heterogeneity. These are key determinants of the types of social action that emerge in cities. To Redfield and others, the transition from rural life to urban settings has a dramatic effect on individuals. They have to learn new ways of coping with their physical environments and with the people who surround them. There is a transition from closely knit rural societies to cities where many people are strangers. This creates difficulties in maintaining certain basic social values and forms of social control.

The emphasis on change from preindustrial to industrial societies provides one form of comparison. The expansion of cities to include suburban and exurban areas provides another. The contrasts in living environments and the life styles that emerge in these different settlements provide us with bases for isolating the processes that bring about urban change and those that are unique to certain types of settlements.

Competition

The "subsocial" school of ecology was developed by Robert Park, Ernest Burgess, and R.D. McKenzie (1925) to study the city in its temporal and spatial dimensions. They set out to explain the resulting patterns in terms of subsocial or "ecological" variables. What emerged from this school were a variety of models of the city that were constructed using an analogy from biology. This analogy assumed that the city develops through "natural" competition affecting growth and development, in a manner similar to growth in biological organisms. This school of thought had a powerful influence for many years on the way in which people studied cities. It has been especially influential in the area of urban planning with its emphasis on spatial distribution of social groups.

The "ecological complex" approach was developed by ecologists who came after Park, Burgess and McKenzie such as Duncan and Schnore (1959). They argued that the major outcomes of city development are brought about by the interaction of four variables: environment, population, social organization, and technology. This approach incorporates the features of the technological, environmental, and subsocial schools into one integrated model of urban development. Using a structural perspective, evaluation has concentrated on the impact of major industrial or commercial change on parts of the urban environment. The emphasis on a global model provides researchers with the ability to assess the total costs and benefits of development in all sectors of the social, physical, economic, and political environments.

The "economic" school focusses on the division of labour in society and its effects on urban social structure. The results of the analysis produced by this perspective include a description of social areas of the city defined by the social characteristics (such as income, ethnicity, and family status) of the inhabitants. Urban social profiles provided the means for identifying the consequences of social change in society. This was represented by spatial allocation throughout the city. The competition for desirable living arrangements between income or ethnic groups could then be monitored through this approach.

The view that natural competition for scarce resources evolves in cities brings these perspectives together. We will examine how the ecological viewpoint has evolved from the earliest days to its current applications.

Social Choice

The "value-orientation" school focusses on the question of values that people share based on common background, cultural heritage, religion, and socialization. Shared values provide the bases for the development of ethnic or social communities maintained through means of segregation and discrimination. The emphasis on values assumes consensus of goals and objectives within a group. This may appear as life styles, religion, organizational behaviour, or moral outlook. The importance of individual background and the maintenance of social interaction in maintaining these values becomes an essential ingredient in understanding this perspective.

Values lead to action. There are many different ways in which people seek life styles that conform to these values. The choices that they make result in a variety of housing arrangements, recreational pursuits, and employment patterns. It is this choice of life styles that will be the focus of our discussion of values.

Allocation

The "social power" school emphasizes a "special interest" approach, where power becomes the critical explanatory variable in understanding the development of cities (Burke, 1968). Important from this perspective is the question of how people get power. Then, how do they use it within the community to influence the distribution of scarce resources? This point of view has been especially prominent in the recent debates about policymaking and planning in cities and the role that the individual citizen can play in affecting them.

In summary, these major schools of urban sociology examine the factors related to origins of cities, urban transformation, competition, choice, and allocation. Each theoretical perspective has contributed to a better understanding of cities and city life; each has its weaknesses and strengths. We can use these perspectives in the chapters that follow to guide us in synthesizing questions ranging from the historical origin of cities to the bases for new towns. We can outline, as well, the social impact of cities on social life and the importance of values and social power in affecting the distribution of individuals and resources within the urban environment.

Van Vliet (1979) reports that most Canadian urban sociologists would stress human ecology in teaching an urban studies course. Presumably, they would adopt this perspective most often in their professional research, as well. The next choice is a perspective emphasizing the social power point of view (critical sociology). This examines the political power structure as a basis of control of urban social structures. Economic and value orientation perspectives are the next most often chosen area of primary emphasis in teaching and research. All of these approaches will be reviewed in this book.

D. PLAN OF THE BOOK

Drawing from the insights provided by Sjoberg, we will order the discussion in the following pages in order to meet three major objectives. First, we will provide the reader with an understanding of how cities have developed and emerged as prominent forces in human societies. Second, we will introduce him or her to perspectives that explain how the structure and form of cities relate to human behaviour. Third, we will provide the reader with a view of how urban problem-solving takes place and its importance for the future of urban societies.

The book is organized so that a specific theme is covered in each chapter. Each theme will correspond to specific factors in explaining the development of cities, human adaptations to urban environments, or the assessment of urban problem-solving. We will begin in Chapter 2 with an examination of the origins of cities and the factors that led to their emergence. Included in this discussion will be an examination of Canadian urban development and the forces of demographic change that have brought about changes in this society. Chapter 3 will examine the transformation that has resulted from the development of urban settlements. This will be studied in terms of changes in social structure and urban life styles. The change from preindustrial to industrial cities, rural to urban life, urban to suburban developments and recent reverse trends ("back to the city" and "back to the country") will all be addressed in this review.

Chapters 4, 5, and 6 deal with different perspectives on social life in the city. The emphasis in Chapter 4 rests on the importance of "competition" in sorting out social groups in selected areas throughout the city. This perspective includes elements of the subsocial school, the ecological complex school, and the economic school. The focus on competition in all of these theories provides an important pivotal point for comparing the research done in each area with that in the other two. Chapter 5 expands on the view of the value-orientation school through a perspective that focusses on "social choice." Here the sorting of people throughout the city is not seen to occur because of a competitive element in urban living but rather to be based on choice. It is assumed that people choose to live in areas that are matched to what they value both in terms of life style and accommodation.

Chapter 6 presents a third view of urban adaptation which is closely related to the social power school. Based on "allocation," this perspective puts the discussion of urban life into the context of the forces of change which derive from the differential power exerted on urban institutions by different groups in the city. The resulting allocations of services, housing, and security all contribute to the quality of life of urban residents but may do so differentially. The role that decision-makers play in resolving any inequities in this allocation is of particular interest in this discussion.

Chapter 7 focusses on the ways in which researchers can collect and apply data that emphasize competition, choice, and allocation as alternative explanations of the framework of urban social life. Chapter 8 summarizes the discussion and proposes some questions for future urban research and urban policy that should be pursued in the effort to create better cities in which to live.

We have taken as our special focus in this book the case of Canadian cities. Wherever appropriate, Canadian research and examples will be cited. This approach allows us to discover where the commonalities in cities appear. It allows for the test of relevancy of theoretical perspectives when applied to Canada. It also provides us with the ability to discuss the unique character of Canadian cities using examples that are familiar to people living in these environments.

E. SUMMARY AND CONCLUSIONS

Cities are often viewed as having unique characteristics, even to the point of assuming human traits. Faced with this, the researcher must distinguish the features of cities that are common to all urban settlements. To do this a systematic approach must be developed in research. The general processes of urbanism and urbanization provide a focus for such an approach.

Urban researchers set down questions that need answers. These questions, or hypotheses, provide the bases for data collection. They bring together concepts to form theories about urban growth and change. Sjoberg (1970:87-100) identifies eight theoretical approaches that have developed over the years. Each of these theories emphasizes different factors in explaining urban processes. We will use this outline to cover different dimensions of the urban experience.

We will examine the bases for the origins of cities and the role that technology and demographic change play in urbanization. We will then study urban change using three perspectives. These perspectives synthesize the theoretical perspectives identified by Sjoberg. They emphasize, specifically, competition, choice, and allocation.

The perspectives that we will examine are developed through the insights provided by research. This involves problem-solving. According to Cohen, the problems related to disgovernance in cities pose the research agenda for contemporary urban researchers. These problems derive from the scale and expanse of cities; from bureaucratization; from political powerlessness; and from conflicts in values. We will be dealing with each of these problems, in turn, when we examine the changes in cities and the effects of competition, choice, and allocation on urban life.

Basic to these concerns are the problems related to income, ethnicity, and family status differences of the urban populations. The characteristics of people in cities are important in predicting their adjustment to urban living. The analysis that follows will show how these relate to poverty, housing shortages, crime, and other forms of social problems.

2 The Origin and Evolution of Cities

A. FACTORS LEADING TO THE ORIGIN OF CITIES

Ecology and Social Structure

Before we can understand the impact that cities have on contemporary society, we must begin by studying their origins and reasons for existence. Cities have evolved through an interaction between physical and social structures. What changes did the evolution of cities bring to the societies of which they were a part? Also, what changes did the societies bring to the cities? We can begin to answer these questions by dealing first with the factors bringing about the emergence of urban settlements.

Before we talk about the origins of cities we should first specify what constitutes an urban place. Golden (1981:28) states that the aspects of settlements which define a place as being urban are permanence, population size, and compactness. An urban place, then, is a relatively permanent settlement of considerable size and density, where density relates to the compact nature of permanent dwellings over a large area.

Now what factors contributed to create cities in the first place? Sjoberg (1970) states that the origins of cities were a function of a social structure that managed the distribution of surpluses provided by technological innovation in agriculture. Technology refers to the sources of energy, the tools, and the know-how applied to the production of goods and services. Variation in levels of technological sophistication provides a useful way of differentiating the steps in societal evolution (Sjoberg, 1970).

The folk, or preliterate, society is characterized by hunting and gathering or foraging. There are small, homogeneous, self-sufficient groups lacking any real division of labour or class system. No cities are associated with such preliterate, folk societies. At this stage, settlements were no more than a few houses gathered together to shelter farmers working their fields. The first cities came when, with developing technology, the hunters and gatherers and the subsistence farmers were able to produce more than they could eat themselves.

Food Surpluses and Technology

Chief among the technological advances that provided the conditions for urban life was the domestication of grains. (Tilly, 1975:43). This occurred first with wheat and barley in the Near and Middle East and northern China, and corn (or maize) in Meso-America (Sjoberg, 1960:29). Grains acted as a concentrated food supply that could be stored over long periods of time. This allowed for a year-round food supply to feed urban populations. Accompanying the development of grains were other technological developments such as animal husbandry, metallurgy, the wheel, the plow, and large-scale irrigation works.

As Adams (1960:154) describes it, the river valley agriculture of Mesopotamia produced crops of wheat and barley which were supplemented by prodigious and dependable supplies of dates and fish. Animals such as sheep, donkeys, and pigs were also available for food. Irrigation had been developed with large-scale canal networks supplying water to fields.

Adams (1960:157) points out that there were three major inducements for Mesopotamian urbanization. First, there was an increased productivity of irrigation agriculture which provided the food surpluses. Second, the practice of irrigation created inequalities in access to productive land. This meant that a stratification system developed according to the volume of grain that individual farmers could reap from the crops. Third, the complexity of these new subsistence pursuits led to a need for institutions to mediate between the conflicting demands of herdsmen and cultivators; fishermen and sailors; plowmakers and plowmen. The surplus of food, in addition, released substantial numbers of people from food production. This allowed them, in turn, to get involved in other activities, such as trade, war, manufacturing, or administration.

As food surpluses appeared, they came to be concentrated and controlled by a small elite. As a result of this control, the elite developed important political power. They also attracted to them, usually in nonagricultural settlements, full time specialists in crafts, government, or economy. These specialized activities fed on one another. The settlements that formed around the elite were crossroads of skills and goods. These activities together contributed to migration into these habitations.

B. THE EARLY CITIES

We have identified the factors that brought about the origins of cities. Now, how did cities differ from other forms of settlement, such as villages and towns? Childe (1970) puts forth ten criteria which he argues serve to distinguish the earliest cities from villages and other such early settlements. First, the early cities were more extensive and more densely populated than any previous settlements. Early cities in Sumeria, for example, had populations ranging from 7,000 to 20,000, which were considerable in early times. Most people were still living in sparsely populated rural areas, relying on hunting and gathering for subsistence.

Second, the composition and function of the urban population differed from that of any village. Many different people gathered in these cities from various parts of the country. In addition to the peasants who still worked the land adjacent to the cities, other classes of people appeared. These included the craftsmen, transport workers, merchants, officials, and priests. All of these people were supported by the agricultural surplus produced by the peasants. Distinctions according to skills and occupation led to the emergence of class differences in cities. These proved more complicated than simply a division according to ruler and ruled. The unskilled peasants, the semi-skilled transportation workers, the skilled craftsmen, the merchants, the intellectuals and priests, the administrators, and the rulers created a hierarchical structure not evident in rural societies.

Third, peasants paid over their surplus from the harvest as a tithe or tax to a lord or king who concentrated this surplus. This led to the creation of a pool of effective capital that could be used for purposes other than supporting agricultural workers. It also required the development of complex systems of tax collection and accounting. A new class of workers emerged, as a result, to serve the ruler.

Fourth, monumental buildings were built with the capital concentrated in the hands of the king and his supporters. These buildings served to symbolize the concentration of social surplus and the power that goes with the ability to control a large pool of labour. Included were temples, massive tombs, and fortresses. These structures developed as areas of sanctuary, as symbols of wealth and power, and as symbols of religious significance. The tombs of the pharaohs, the castles of the crusader knights, and the palaces of the European kings were all a product of concentrated wealth and a need to impress on people the power of the ruling elite.

Fifth, all of those people not involved in food production were supported in the first instance by the surplus accumulated in the temples or royal granaries. They were thus dependent on the priests or court for favours. The concentration of surplus in the hands of a few led to the development of a ruling class exempt from all manual tasks. The lower classes were, in return, guaranteed peace and security. They were also relieved from any intellectual activity. Planning and organization were left to the ruling class.

Sixth, the administration of these societies led to the need for means of recording and documenting revenues. Writing systems evolved to provide consistent and understandable means of achieving this end. The development of tax records, the communication of laws, and the inscription of religious tracts all depended on writing. Few people learned to write, and those who did formed an important class in the society. Most often, it was the priests who acquired this skill. They used the ability to decipher important documents, records, and religious tracts as an important basis for power in the social structure. They, in turn, provided legitimacy to the ruler. This ensured his hold on the surplus provided by the peasants.

Seventh, the invention of writing had other effects on these societies, as well. It allowed scholars to elaborate on the exact and predictive sciences — arithmetic, geometry, and astronomy. The development of calendars and means of recording time facilitated the regulation of the successive cycles of agricultural operations. This enhancement of scientific technology led, of course, to the development of even greater surpluses. It also provided the means of protecting these surpluses. Through the development of metallurgy, for example, weapons of war became more sophisticated and more powerful.

Eighth, other specialists who were also supported by the concentration of social surplus were free to give vent to artistic expression. Full time artisans went to work creating art forms — sculpted, painted, or carved — without concerning themselves with who would provide their next meal. This artistic explosion was very much a function of patronage. The need to go to cities to find this support from the rulers in the society swelled the urban settlements even more.

Ninth, the concentrated surplus allowed the importation of raw materials needed for industry but not locally available. Foreign trade developed. With this exchange of materials came the interchange of ideas among cities. Crossroads along trade routes or natural harbours became logical places for the trading of goods and formed the centres of commerce for large hinterland areas. The great traders and warriors of early times, such as the Phoenicians, Romans, and Greeks, travelled the waters of the Mediterranean. They built cities from one end of the sea to the other, as trading centres and fortresses of military might. The Greek and Roman cities that appeared in the southern coast of Turkey, for example, had forums for 10,000 people to gather at one time. These people were involved in commerce and administrative control of these territories.

The continued growth of cities was often a function, then, of their location. Many cities were situated on rivers, lakes or seas, where trade and commerce was made easier through the passage of boats along natural waterways. The importance of trade and commerce in city development and growth continues today. It is now roadways and airline routes that influence urban growth.

Tenth, specialist craftsmen were both provided with raw materials needed for the employment of their skills and guaranteed security based on residence rather than kinship. The city was a community to which a craftsman could belong politically, as well as economically.

The emergence of cities, then, related to (1) the evolution of technology; (2) the development of social organizations to manage agricultural surplus and to legitimize existing authority; (3) the importation of skills and goods into a central area to be controlled and distributed throughout the society in a way that maintained central authority; and (4) the development of physical structures that gave body to social structure.

The early cities which formed in this way were found mainly in Mesopotamia, the Nile Valley, China, and Mesoamerica. In these places, the ecology and the climate combined to provide inhabitants with the ability to create surpluses. At first, there were small politically independent city-states where people shared a common language, religion, social organization, and material culture. Because of the difficulties of transportation, there were very limited hinterlands under the control of these cities (Sjoberg, 1960:34).

Each city was ruled by a king who represented the local deity and was its chief priest. As the land and crops were held in trust to this deity, the king demanded a part of the surplus crop as payment. The king and his administration lived within walled fortifications around a temple to the god(s).

As an example, Farb (1968) describes the basis for growth of the large cities of the Aztecs in Mexico. In the central area of the country, called the Valley of Mexico, there was once a 3,000 square mile basin of water surrounded by mountains. To control the valley, the Aztecs first had to control the water resource. They developed for this purpose an agricultural technique employing narrow strips of land (chinampas) surrounded by a network of canals. These chinampas produced several crops a year and remained fertile for centuries because of the constant replenishing with soil taken from the beds of the canals.

With the surpluses of food produced by this agricultural system, the Aztecs were able to erect a capital city which, in the 1500s, had a population of 200,000 to 300,000 people. This was several times the size of London in the same period (Farb, 1968:170). The capital, Tenochtitlán, had centrally located temples and a great pyramid. This was testament to the wealth and authority of the king and the religious leaders. An extensive roadway system was developed to tie the city to the surrounding countryside. This allowed commerce and trade to move easily into and out of the city.

When Cortez first saw Tenochtitlán in 1519, it had narrow canals as in Venice and three main avenues. The dwellings of the nobles were of pink stone, and included courtyards with fountains, birds, and flowers. An aqueduct brought fresh water to the city (Hayner, 1968:168).

This beautiful city was completely destroyed by the Spaniards. The revival of the city in this century to the massive scale of today's Mexico City shows the importance of social, political, and economic factors combining to create and sustain a major urban area.

C. CANADIAN URBAN DEVELOPMENT

The development of Canadian settlements followed similar stages to those of early cities. An area previously supporting hunting and gathering was settled by societies that were more advanced technologically. The colonizers relied on trade in such staple commodities as furs, and in agricultural surpluses.

The establishment of a wintering fur depot and trading post at Tadoussac in 1600 marked the first step toward colonial settlement in Canada (Nader, 1975:156). By 1663, New France had only 2,500 colonists, half of them living in Québec, Montréal, and Trois Rivières. By 1698, these three towns constituted 22 percent of the population of 15,355 in New France. Québec, because of its role as the political, cultural, institutional, and military capital of a colony with a highly centralized bureaucracy, attracted the largest population. At that time, Canada in general could hardly be described as urbanized.

With the transition from French to English rule, the focus of the Canadian economy turned from the fur trade to agriculture. Immigration from Britain and from the United States made possible the development of agricultural settlements further inland, in the Eastern Townships and on Lake Ontario. With this expansion of agriculture inland, Montréal took over from Québec as the preeminent Canadian city. By the early 1800s, it was the main marketplace of Canada. Here were located the principal wholesalers and importers for both the fur trade and the growing agricultural settlements (Nader, 1975:163).

With the designation of Upper Canada as a province in 1791, there was a need to choose an administrative capital and military base for the new province. Niagara was the location of the first parliament but its proximity to the United States made it vulnerable to attack. After much deliberation by the English military, York (present-day Toronto) was selected over London and Kingston as the capital. The choice of York was made because of its good harbour and its easy access across land to Georgian Bay and Lake Huron. Toronto's ascendancy as the commercial and political centre of Upper Canada was assured from that point onward.

After the mid-1830s Hamilton's rapid growth as an industrial centre was spurred on by access to cheap Pennsylvania coal delivered along the Welland Canal. Ottawa's early development was based on the lumber industry, with access to markets provided by the Rideau Canal. London, meanwhile, grew as a service centre to the agricultural areas of Southwestern Ontario. Its growth was also due to its central location on the Great Western Railway, which was begun in 1851. Niagara declined as a centre when the Welland Canal bypassed the town, thereby encouraging growth in St. Catharines instead (Nader, 1975:177).

In the Maritimes, early settlement occurred in Halifax as it became, in 1749, the political, commercial, and military capital of Nova Scotia. The growth of sea trade helped Halifax maintain this position up to the time of Confederation. St. John, New Brunswick meanwhile grew on sawmilling and shipbuilding. The fisheries in Newfoundland created and promoted the growth of St. John's (Nader, 1975:194).

The settlement of the Canadian West started at Point Douglas (now part of Winnipeg) with one hundred settlers arriving in 1812 to found the Red River Colony. The real growth happened around Fort Garry where, in the 1830s, fur trading brought a colony of 3,000 to the confluence of the Assiniboine and Red Rivers. The importance of the fur trade in the West led to the establishment of trading posts such as Fort Carleton and Fort Edmonton.

In the mid-1800s, the transCanada railway brought people to the West to farm and returned to the East with agricultural produce. The settlements, such as Calgary and Regina, built up around the railroad stations also provided markets and service areas for the surrounding areas. The coming of the railway tied together Pacific coastal settlements. These had previously relied on contact with the United States and the Orient. They were now merged into a growing Canadian urban system.

Thus, Canadian experience with urban settlement reflects the many different reasons for the location and growth of cities in general. Economic factors based on proximity to markets and commodities; political factors determined by the need for administrative control over a society; military factors related to security; and social factors resulting in large-scale immigration have all contributed to the development of Canadian cities.

D. DEMOGRAPHIC CHANGE AND URBAN GROWTH

When we look beyond the issue of city origins, we have to address the question of how cities continue to grow. The consideration of sources of population growth becomes important. Here, the concern is less with the changes in the social or physical structure of society which lead to variations in settlement patterns and more with the consequences of these changes in demographic terms.

Davis (1974:165) points out that cities can become larger due to three specific principles of demographic change. First of all, the proportion of people in cities can rise because rural settlements grow larger and are reclassified as towns or cities. Second, the excess of births over deaths, "natural increase," may be greater in the city than in the country, causing city populations to swell. Third, people may move from the country to the city to cause urban growth. This migration may occur either from inside a nation or through immigration from outside.

Reclassification

Davis claims that the first factor, "reclassification," usually has only a small influence on urbanization. However, through annexations, some small towns are absorbed by cities and are subsequently redefined as urban. In the Canadian experience with reclassification,

Figure 2.1
Average Percentage Change of Population Within All CMAs, 1971-1976

Per cent

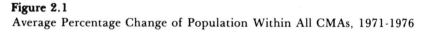
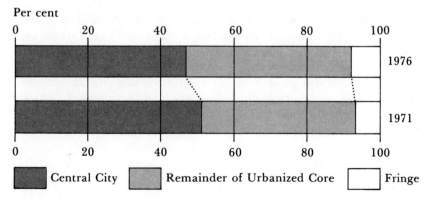

Source: Statistics Canada, *Canada's Cities*. Ottawa: Statistics Canada, Chart 7, 1980.
Reproduced by permission of the Minister of Supply and Services Canada.

the rapid growth of metropolitan areas has led to uneven distribution of population between cities and suburbs. The extent of this suburban growth in recent years is outlined in Figure 2.1.

As cities grew, the core areas found it increasingly difficult to encompass all of the population which they serviced either through employment or through other amenities. The deliberate movement to suburban areas to escape the costs of the big city services, congestion, and land costs left cities without adequate financial resources to meet the needs of their residents.

Many of these suburban communities have strongly resisted "urban reform" that would mean their incorporation into the larger city through annexation. Several strategies have been adopted in Canada to resolve the inequities of suburban growth and increased city costs. The most common solution has been the development of metropolitan level governments, discussed above, where services are shared across all communities. However, such things as planning remain the responsibility of each of the incorporated cities within their own boundaries.

Annexation has been used to increase the jurisdiction of cities. In 1961, Calgary was allowed to annex large areas of surrounding countryside, including the city of Bowness, Forest Lawn, Montgomery, and parts of the municipal districts of Foothills and Rocky View. Calgary has since maintained a policy of incorporating small settlements which lie beyond its boundaries into the city and concentrating growth within its jurisdiction (Bettison, et al., 1975:38).

Edmonton, on the other hand, has been characterized as a compact centre with identifiable satellite communities beyond its borders. A recent attempt by the City of Edmonton to annex communities outside of its boundaries met vigorous resistance. As a result, it was not successful in achieving its main objective of annexing Sherwood Park and St. Albert (about 70,000 people) into the larger urban area. In terms of definitions, the people who live in the City of St. Albert consitute an urban population so their status would not have changed with annexation. Sherwood Park is still classified as a hamlet, however. Its residents are not strictly urban even though this community is little more than a suburb of Edmonton. Edmonton did grow a bit as a result of the annexation bid, however. Still, reclassification added only 9,547 people to the city in 1981 (a 1.7 percent increase). This compares with an overall increase for that year of 5.8 percent or 30,109 people.

Natural Increase

Natural increase, the second principle of demographic change outlined by Davis, is also insignificant in bringing about urbanization. Cities rarely have higher levels than rural areas. A chief obstacle to the growth of cities in the past has been their excessive mortality rates (Davis, 1974:166). As Gillis (1980:524) points out, disease (and more significantly the Black Death) had a deurbanizing effect on the European population during the Middle Ages. The problems of overcrowding, poor sanitary conditions, and poor working conditions concentrated the causes of disease. This raised the mortality rates among urban dwellers. When many of these problems were brought under control in the last century, other factors went to work to lower the fertility rates in cities although they remained high in rural areas. These factors included changing attitudes towards birth control and the woman's role in society. Women became essential members of the labour force. This led to an increased incidence of smaller nuclear families. This trend continues today with modern suburban families remaining smaller than rural families. At the same time, in Canada, not only have birth rates been higher in rural than in urban areas since 1921, but death rates are still lower in hamlets and farms than in cities (Gertler and Crowley, 1977:67).

Rural-Urban Migration

Davis (1974:167) claims that the main source of growth in urban areas is rural-urban migration. As a nation's industrial productivity grows (as it moves from a preindustrial to an industrial economy), services and manufacturing require more manpower. People are attracted out of rural areas, where mechanization reduces the demand for labour. They go off in search of the higher wages found in the industrial plants in the cities.

The Industrial Revolution in Britain coincided with a dramatic increase in population through natural increase. But it was migration that had the most significant effect on British urban society. Highly populated rural areas lost population to the northern counties, whose coal and iron resources attracted industry. These areas became major centres of population overnight. The new factories involved in textile production alone, which had employed 57,000 workers in 1818, had half a million employees by 1840 (Pawley, 1971:10). Added to the attraction of work in cities was the pressure of land enclosures. For the sake of agricultural efficiency of large farms, small landholders were forced out of the rural areas.

In Canada, industrialization came much later and more slowly than in Britain. Between 1871 and 1901, the proportion of the population residing in incorporated cities, towns, and villages increased from 18.3 to 34.9 percent. In the decade from 1901 to 1911, both the urban and rural populations grew with large numbers of immigrants arriving to populate the cities and to farm the Prairies. During this period the rural population dropped from 65.1 to 58.2

percent, with increases in the population size coming at only one-third the rate experienced in the cities (Kalbach and McVey, 1979:136). The movement towards an urbanized population had begun.

Canada reached an even balance between numbers of rural and urban dwellers during the 1930s. World War II gave further impetus to urbanization, especially with the importance that industrialization of the economy gained in this period and afterward. The dominance of the urban areas over the rural, in terms of growth, is illustrated in Figure 2.2. Especially in the period from 1930 to 1960, urban growth has been much greater than rural.

Figure 2.2

Intercensal Rate of Urban and Rural Population Growth, Canada, 1901-1976

Percentage Change

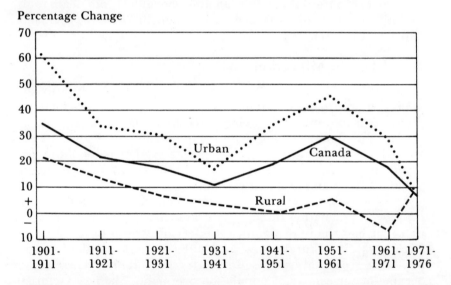

Source: Statistics Canada, *Canada's Cities*. Ottawa: Statistics Canada, Chart 1, 1980.
Reproduced by permission of the Minister of Supply and Services Canada.

Immigration

Another form of migration, immigration, also contributed to urban growth in Canada. Immigrants tend to choose cities as their primary destination when coming to Canada for reasons of employment (increasingly so today). The major recipients of these immigrants are Toronto, then Montreal and Vancouver. This selectivity among immigrants for certain cities is underlined by the fact that in the decade 1951-61 all metropolitan areas in Canada grew at a rate of

45 percent. However, over one fourth (26.9 percent) of all post-World War II immigrants still residing in Canada at the time of the 1961 census were living in Toronto, 14.2 percent in Montreal, and 6.6 percent in Vancouver. In other words, at that time, these three centres combined accounted for just less than half of all foreign-born people in Canada (Kalbach and McVey, 1979:144).

Just under 40 percent of the foreign-born living in Canada who had arrived prior to 1961 were British. However, the proportion of British in the immigrant population dropped to 19 percent in 1977-1978. This was in part a result of significant increases in the immigrant proportions of Italians and other Southern Europeans, and of Asian and non-European groups. The proportion of Asian and other non-European origin immigrants who had immigrated prior to 1961 and were still living in Canada in 1971 was just under three percent. For those who had arrived in Canada between 1961 and 1971, the proportion was 17 percent (Kalbach and McVey, 1979:60).

As pointed out above, these waves of immigrants provided the major source of growth in Canadian cities. An important consideration with these immigrant groups may be the retention of their culture. Social and physical boundaries based on ethnic differences may develop in urban areas. A study done by Richmond (1974) in the Toronto area (quoted in Kalbach and McVey, 1979) indicated that immigrants adapt to the "host" society in different ways. He found that one third of the immigrants were assimilated into the majority "Anglo" society. Ten percent were partially integrated but maintained ethnic ties. Seventeen percent, because of their high social and physical mobility, did not develop any real permanent ties to Canadian society. Another third formed ethnic compounds in the city, a manifestation of the building of cultural boundaries through physical isolation (Kalbach and McVey, 1979:61).

Within these boundaries, the language and traditions of the homeland are maintained in resistance to the host society. The implications of this boundary maintenance include the positive aspects of cultural diversity in cities. The negative aspects revolve around the friction that is created as a result of suspicion and misunderstandings that develop between immigrant groups and others in the city. These consequences of immigration will be examined in detail further in the discussion of the ecology of cities and the bases of choice in urban location.

Recent Migration Trends

Table 2.1 presents a composite picture of the contribution that natural increase and immigration have made to the growth of Canada's population in the years from 1851 to 1976. Of note in this table are the large levels of net migration in the years from 1901 to 1921 and again from 1951 to 1976. As mentioned above, most of this immigration ended up in the cities, serving as a major source of their growth. Natural increase has been a major factor contributing to Canada's population growth. However, in recent years its importance has diminished, reflecting dropping rates of Canadian fertility.

Table 2.1.
Growth components of Canada's population, 1851-1976[1]

Period	Total population growth '000	Births '000	Deaths '000	Natural increase '000	Ratio of natural increase to total growth %	Immigration '000	Emigration '000	Net migration '000	Ratio of net migration to total growth %	Population at the end of the census period '000
1851-1861	793	1,281	670	611	77.0	352	170	182	23.0	3,230
1861-1871	460	1,370	760	610	132.6	260	410	-150	-32.6	3,689
1871-1881	636	1,480	790	690	108.5	350	404	-54	-8.5	4,325
1881-1891	508	1,524	870	654	128.7	680	826	-146	-28.7	4,833
1891-1901	538	1,548	880	668	124.2	250	380	-130	-24.2	5,371
1901-1911	1,835	1,925	900	1,025	55.9	1,550	740	810	44.1	7,207
1911-1921	1,581	2,340	1,070	1,270	80.3	1,400	1,089	311	19.7	8,788
1921-1931	1,589	2,420	1,060	1,360	85.5	1,200	970	230	14.5	10,377
1931-1941	1,130	2,294	1,072	1,222	108.1	149	241	-92	-8.1	11,507
1941-1951[2]	2,503	3,212	1,220	1,992	92.3	548	382	166	7.7	14,009
1951-1956	2,071	2,106	633	1,473	71.1	783	185	598	28.9	16,081
1956-1961	2,157	2,362	687	1,675	77.7	760	278	482	22.3	18,238
1961-1966	1,777	2,249	731	1,518	85.4	539	280	259	14.6	20,015
1966-1971	1,553	1,856	766	1,090	70.2	890	427	463	29.8	21,568
1971-1976	1,424	1,756	822	934	65.6	841	351	490	34.4	22,993

[1]Includes Newfoundland since 1951.
[2]Data on growth components shown for 1941-51 were obtained by including data for Newfoundland for 1949-50 and 1950-51 only.
Source: Statistics Canada. *Canada Year Book 1978-79*. Ottawa: Statistics Canada. Table 4.2. Reproduced by permission of the Minister of Supply and Services Canada.

The concentration of population in Canadian cities resulting from natural increase, rural-urban migration, and immigration can be illustrated in two ways. Figure 2.3 shows the geographic distribution of people in census metropolitan areas as of 1976. Statistics Canada (1981:VII) defines an urban place as having a population concentration of 1,000 or more and a population density of 400 or more per square kilometre. Obviously, in the category of urban there are wide variations according to the size of the population. Recognizing this, there is a distinction made between towns, villages, small cities, and census metropolitan areas (CMA). The

CMA is the main labour market area of a continuous built-up area having a population of 100,000 or more. A CMA comprises : (1) municipalities completely or partly inside an urbanized core; and (2) other municipalities lying outside the urbanized core if (a) at least 40 percent of the employed labour force living in the municipality works in the urbanized core, or (b) at least 25 percent of the employed labour force working in the municipality lives in the urbanized core (Statistics Canada, 1981:X). In 1981, there were 24 CMAs in Canada.

Figure 2.3   Population Distribution by Census Metropolitan Areas, 1976

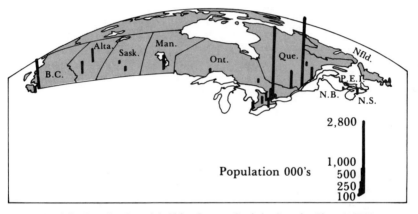

Source: Statistics Canada, *Canada's Cities*. Ottawa: Statistics Canada, Chart 4, 1980.
Reproduced by permission of the Minister of Supply and Services Canada.

Figure 2.4 shows an isodemographic map which illustrates population concentration in a different way. This map displays the number of people in an area as a proportion of the total population in the country. A city of one million people is twice as large on the map as a city of 500,000 people. The heavy population concentration in the industrial corridor between Montreal and Toronto compared to the cities in the West, for example, is dramatically illustrated in this map.

Rural-urban migration was still taking place in 1971, even though the level of urbanization in Canada was very high. Of the 3,581,725 migrants living in Canada in 1966, and who were still in Canada in 1971, 585,130 had moved to a more urban location, i.e. from rural farm or rural non-farm to urban places or from farm to non-farm areas. At the same time, 562,095 had moved to a more rural area, resulting in a net urbanward movement for that period of only 25,035 (Kalbach and McVey, 1979:138). The largest pro-

Figure 2.4   Concentration of Population in Canadian Cities

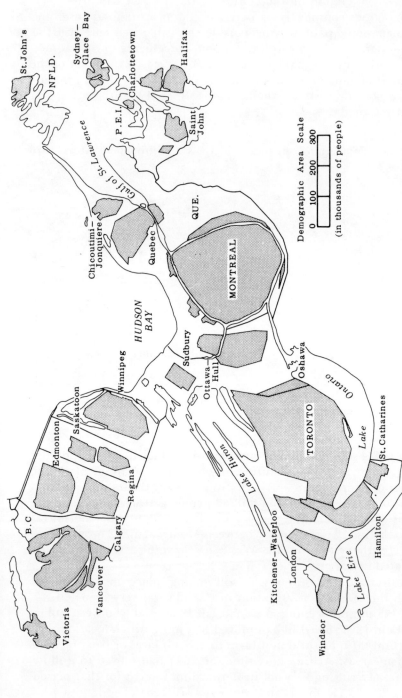

Sources: L. Skoda and C.I. Jackson. "A Mechanical Method of Constructing Equal Population Density Maps." Discussion Paper 8.72.4 (Ottawa Ministry of State for Urban Affairs (MSUA), 1972) and L. Skoda and J.C. Robertson, *Isodemographic Map of Canada*, Department of Environment, Geographical Paper No. 50 (Ottawa Information Canada, 1972). Reproduced by permission of the Minister of Supply and Services Canada.

portion of these urban to rural movers had moved from urban to rural nonfarm areas.

Looking at the figures for 1976 (see Table 2.2), 803,925 people who were living in a CMA or Census Agglomeration (CA) in 1971 moved to a non-CMA or less urban place. At the same time, 702,530 people who were living in a non-CMA place moved to a CMA or CA. This resulted in a net ruralward movement of 101,395. Of course, cities still expanded with their attractiveness to immigrants.

Table 2.2.
Migrant population 5 years and over, by locality of residence in 1971 and 1976

| Locality of residence in 1971 | Locality of residence in 1976 | | | Total |
	Census metropolitan areas	Census agglomeration	Non-census metropolitan areas	migrants (by residence in 1971)
Census metropolitan areas (CMA)[1]	1,546,935	155,255	620,665	2,322,855
Census agglomeration (CA)[1]	163,915	116,730	183,260	463,910
Non-CMA or non-CA	511,235	191,295	872,690	1,575,220
Outside Canada	575,530	37,575	106,570	719,675
Residence of CMA or CA unknown	139,830	25,225	77,305	242,360
Total migrants[2] (by residence in 1976)	2,937,450	526,085	1,860,490	5,324,025

[1] As defined for the 1976 Census.
[2] Excludes persons in the armed forces or in other government service, stationed outside Canada.
Source: Statistics Canada, Canada Year Book 1978-79. Ottawa: Statistics Canada. Table 4.67.
Reproduced by permission of the Minister of Supply and Services Canada.

This move into rural areas is being referred to as the "population turnaround," a phenomenon which is occurring not only in Canada but also in the U.S. In this migration, people are moving to rural areas to retire, for job opportunities, or to get away from big city congestion and cost. We will discuss this in detail in the next chapter.

A National Urban System

In summary, it was not until the 1920s that a truly national urban system developed in Canada (Nader, 1975:211). Prime agricultural land was, for the most part, under cultivation. A strong manufacturing industry had been established. With the expansion in the demand for urban services and communication technology, the means were developed for integrating the widely scattered metropolitan centres across Canada into one. The advent of the telephone after 1900 allowed concentration of head offices in urban centres, while maintaining control over hinterland areas. The automobile, as well, promoted the growth of metropolitan economic regions.

Despite the growth of urban settlements and their importance as commercial, military, and political centres Canada stayed a predominantly rural society until the middle of this century. In 1930, 50 percent of Canada's population still lived in rural areas (see Figure 2.5).

Figure 2.5
Percentage of Urban Population of Canada and Regions, 1851-1971

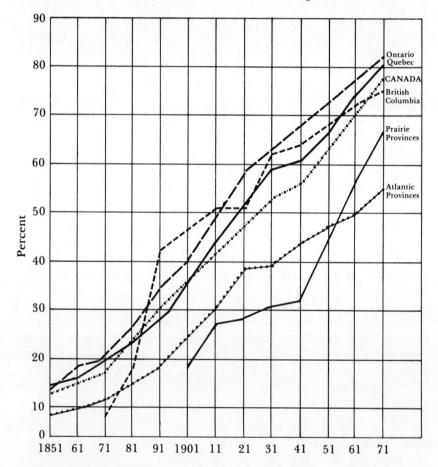

Source: M.V. George, *Population Growth in Canada*, 1971 Census of Canada, V (Part 1), p. 45. Reproduced by permission of the Minister of Supply and Services Canada.

Table 2.3.
Urban and Rural Population, for Canada, Provinces and Territories Showing
Percentage Change 1976-1981

	1976[1]		1981		Percentage Change 1976-81
Canada	22,992,604	(100.0)	24,343,181	(100.0)	5.9
urban	17,566,196	(76.4)	18,435,927	(75.7)	5.0
rural	5,426,408	(23.6)	5,907,254	(24.3)	8.9
Newfoundland	557,725	(100.0)	567,681	(100.0)	1.8
urban	331,504	(59.4)	332,898	(58.6)	0.4
rural	226,221	(40.6)	234,783	(41.4)	3.8
Prince Edward Island	118,229	(100.0)	122,506	(100.0)	3.6
urban	46,346	(39.2)	44,515	(36.3)	−4.0
rural	71,883	(60.8)	77,991	(63.7)	8.5
Nova Scotia	828,571	(100.0)	847,442	(100.0)	2.3
urban	468,155	(56.6)	466,842	(55.1)	−0.3
rural	360,416	(43.4)	380,600	(44.9)	5.6
New Brunswick	677,250	(100.0)	696,403	(100.0)	2.8
urban	362,479	(53.5)	353,220	(50.7)	−2.6
rural	314,771	(46.5)	343,183	(49.3)	9.0
Québec	6,234,445	(100.0)	6,438,403	(100.0)	3.3
urban	4,966,316	(79.6)	4,993,839	(77.5)	0.6
rural	1,268,129	(20.4)	1,444,564	(22.5)	13.9
Ontario	8,264,465	(100.0)	8,625,107	(100.0)	4.4
urban	6,771,309	(81.9)	7,047,032	(81.7)	4.1
rural	1,493,156	(18.1)	1,578,075	(18.3)	5.7
Manitoba	1,021,506	(100.0)	1,026,241	(100.0)	0.5
urban	726,253	(71.1)	730,659	(71.2)	0.6
rural	295,253	(28.9)	295,582	(28.8)	0.1
Saskatchewan	921,323	(100.0)	968,313	(100.0)	5.1
urban	514,627	(55.9)	563,166	(58.2)	9.4
rural	406,696	(44.1)	405,147	(41.8)	−0.4
Alberta	1,838,037	(100.0)	2,237,724	(100.0)	21.7
urban	1,393,486	(75.8)	1,727,545	(77.2)	24.0
rural	444,551	(24.2)	510,179	(22.8)	14.8
British Columbia	2,466,608	(100.0)	2,744,467	(100.0)	11.3
urban	1,951,247	(79.1)	2,139,412	(78.0)	9.6
rural	515,361	(20.9)	605,055	(22.0)	17.4
Yukon	21,836	(100.0)	23,153	(100.0)	6.0
urban	13,311	(61.0)	14,814	(64.0)	11.3
rural	8,525	(39.0)	8,339	(36.0)	−2.2
Northwest Territories	42,609	(100.0)	45,741	(100.0)	7.4
urban	21,163	(49.7)	21,985	(48.1)	3.9
rural	21,446	(50.3)	23,756	(51.9)	10.8

[1] *Based on 1981 area and definition.*
The figures in brackets represent the population count as a percentage of the total population.
Source: *Statistics Canada Daily*, Tuesday, June 15, 1982, p. 6.
Reproduced by permission of the Minister of Supply and Services Canada.

Since 1950, Canada's population has become increasingly urban. In 1981, 75 percent of Canadians lived in cities. In fact, since the end of World War II, Canada's rate of urban growth has been greater than world averages. Projecting to the year 2001, some demographers have estimated that 90-95 percent of Canada's population will be urban dwellers (Gertler and Crowley, 1977:41).

As Nader points out, although metropolitanism has always been a formative force in Canadian urban history, metropolitan dominance has never been as pervasive as it is at present. Metropolitanism implies ". . . the focussing of extensive economic regions upon large urban areas which act as decision-making centres. The metropolis performs a clearing-house function for its region by acting as a forum for a regional viewpoint (e.g. through its newspapers), by organizing the regional economy through control over the alloca-

Table 2.4.
Population for Census Metropolitan Areas, Showing Percentage Change, 1976 and 1981

	1976[1]	1981	Percentage change
Calgary, Alta.	471,397[2]	592,743	25.7
Chicoutimi-Jonquière, Que.	128,643	135,172	5.1
Edmonton, Alta.	556,270[2]	657,057	18.1
Halifax, N.S.	267,991	277,727	3.6
Hamilton, Ont.	529,371	542,095	2.4
Kitchener, Ont.	272,158	287,801	5.8
London, Ont.	270,383	283,668	4.9
Montréal, Que.	2,802,547[2]	2,828,349	0.9
Oshawa, Ont.	135,196	154,217	14.1
Ottawa-Hull, Ont./Que.	693,288	717,978	3.6
Québec, Que.	542,158	576,075	6.3
Regina, Sask.	151,191	164,313	8.7
Saint John, N.B.	112,974	114,048	1.0
Saskatoon, Sask.	133,793[2]	154,210	15.3
St. Catharines-Niagara, Ont.	301,921	304,353	0.8
St. John's, Nfld.	145,400[2]	154,820	6.5
Sudbury, Ont.	157,030	149,923	−4.5
Thunder Bay, Ont.	119,253	121,379	1.8
Toronto, Ont.	2,803,101	2,998,947	7.0
Trois-Rivières, Que.	106,031[2]	111,453	5.1
Vancouver, B.C.	1,166,348	1,268,183	8.7
Victoria, B.C.	218,250	233,481	7.0
Windsor, Ont.	247,582	246,110	−0.6
Winnipeg, Man.	578,217	584,842	1.2

[1] Based on 1981 area.
[2] Adjusted figures due to boundary changes.
Source: *Statistics Canada Daily,* Tuesday, March 30, 1982, p. 3.
Reproduced by permission of the Minister of Supply and Services Canada.

tion of resources (e.g. through its financial institutions and head offices), and by acting as an intermediary agent between the region and other metropolitan areas (e.g. through superior communication facilities)" (Nader, 1975:213).

Table 2.3 presents recent statistics showing the changes in the urban and rural population division by province from 1976 to 1981. The very high levels of urbanization in Ontario, Quebec, Alberta, and British Columbia when compared to the other provinces are well illustrated. Also, there is some growth in the rural areas evident in these statistics but the general trend towards urban living has stayed the same.

Table 2.4 presents figures for population growth from 1976 to 1981 in the Canadian CMAs. Edmonton, Calgary, and Saskatoon show the effects of Westward migration in Canada. This contrasts well with the steady growth (around 7 percent in five years) for Toronto and Vancouver. In that time period, Montreal stopped growing. This table illustrates the effects that internal migration can have on the growth of particular cities. The urbanization process in a country may have different regional effects.

E. WORLD URBANIZATION

According to Golden (1981:68), in 1970 2.2 billion or 61 percent of the total world population of 3.6 billion people were rural. In 1982, these figures were approximately 63 percent of 4.6 billion (United Nations, 1982). This compares with a population in 1981 in Canada which was 24 percent rural. Now, while proportionately there are more rural people in the world, in absolute terms the numbers of urban dwellers are huge. Many of these people live in major cities which are congested and overcrowded with people.

There are about 880,000 villages and 38,000 towns as against approximately 1,780 cities of 100,000 people or more in the world. The typical urban place, therefore, is small — averaging perhaps around 35,000 (Golden, 1981:72). However, of the urban population, 62 percent live in cities over 100,000 (see Table 2.5).

A third of the world's urban population live in metropolitan areas with populations of 1 million and over such as Hong Kong, Cairo, Toronto, Montreal, and New York (see Table 2.6). Large cities are fewer in number than small towns but they contain immense populations. As of 1970, 27 cities had populations over 4 million. Altogether, these cities contained about 190 million people.

In terms of regional distribution of urbanization, these figures reflect world economic and social development. The transformation to worldwide urbanization began in Europe and spread unevenly from there. As a consequence, there is a concentration of high levels of urbanization in particular parts of the world (see Figure 2.6).

Table 2.5.
The Urban Situation in the World, 1950 and 1970

	Population				Urban Population		Number of Places	
	Number (in millions)		Percent		Percent			
	1950	1970	1950	1970	1950	1970	1950	1970
World	2,501	3,628	100.0	100.0	—	—	—	—
Rural	1,796	2,229	71.8	61.4	—	—	—	—
Urban	706	1,399	28.2	38.6	100.0	100.0	24,273	39,771
Town	300	535	12.0	14.8	42.5	38.3	23,311	37,994
City (100,000+)	406	864	16.2	23.8	57.5	61.7	962	1,777
Urban[a]	706	1,399	28.2	38.6	100.0	100.0	24,273	39,771
5,000+	681	1,363	27.2	37.6	96.5	97.4	16,709	28,875
20,000+	567	1,170	22.6	32.2	80.2	83.6	4,973	9,341
100,000+	406	864	16.2	23.8	57.5	61.7	962	1,777
500,000+	255	572	10.2	15.8	36.0	40.9	187	353
1,000,000+	182	448	7.3	12.4	25.7	32.0	79	174
4,000,000+	70	191	2.8	5.2	9.9	13.6	11	27

	Mean Sizes of Places[b]			Size of Place Where Average Dweller Lives[b]	
	1950	1970		1950	1970
All places	416 to 1,375	486 to 1,599	All dwellers	318,000	608,000
Urban places	29,102	35,176	Urban dwellers	1,125,000	1,575,000
Cities	422,056	486,136	City dwellers	1,933,000	2,533,000

Based on data from Kingsley Davis, *World Urbanization 1950-1970*, Vol. II (University of California, Berkeley: Institute of International Studies, 1972), Chapter 2.
[a] Note that these size classes are *open* classes, that is, the class of places 5,000 and over includes the places 20,000 and over, 100,000 and over, and so forth. Hence, these percentages cannot be added up.
[b] These figures are estimates that help to convey the impact on the size of places and on the typical place in which people live of both world population growth and urbanization.
Source: Golden, H.H., *Urbanization and Cities*. Lexington, Mass.: D.C. Heath, Table 4.1.

Very high levels are concentrated in Northern Europe, Australia-New Zealand, North America, Temperate South America, Western Europe, and Japan. Together, these areas contain 17 percent of the world's total population and 34 percent of the world's urban population. However, they also represent less than 7 percent of the world's rural population (Golden, 1981:81).

At the same time, the absolute numbers of people lead to large-scale metropolises developing in less urbanized parts of the world. Asia is the world's most populated region. It contains both the largest proportion of all of the world's cities and the largest proportion of the world's cities with a million or more inhabitants. This occurs with the second lowest (next to Africa) level of overall urbanization.

Their great population pressure has led to some interesting population experiments by the Chinese. There are now official sanctions on having more than one child. This is a direct attempt to reduce the levels of natural increase. Also, internal migration (as well as emigration) is severely curtailed. The mass movement of people from rural to urban areas in China is a thing of the past. Regulations exist which restrict rural people from going into the cities, other than for purposes of trade or as tourists. These combined efforts are expected to stabilize the urban populations and reduce the severe strain that population growth puts on services and facilities in cities.

As we pointed out above, Latin America, unlike China, is experiencing large-scale growth in its cities. By the year 2000, urban centres in this region are expected to contain 500 million people. Nineteen metropolitan areas alone will encompass 250 million, up from just 70 million in 1975 (Turner, 1976:955). Cities are growing at a rate of 4 percent a year, on average. Annually, Latin America's rural population rises by about 1.5 million persons, while its urban areas swell by 7 million. This urban growth is predominantly a function of massive internal migration from rural to urban areas.

Table 2.6.
The World's Urban Population and Places According to Size, 1970[a]

| | | Percentage of | | |
Size Category[b]	Population (in thousands)	World Population	Urban Population	Number of Urban Places
Urban Places				
Total Urban	1,399,000	38.6	100.0	39,771
8,000,000	101,312	2.8	7.2	10
4,000,000	89,504	2.5	6.4	17
2,000,000	111,303	3.1	8.0	43
1,000,000	146,205	4.0	10.5	104
500,000	123,227	3.4	8.8	179
250,000	131,907	3.6	9.4	384
100,000	160,406	4.4	11.4	1,040
50,000	130,409	3.6	9.3	1,844
20,000	175,228	4.8	12.5	5,720
10,000	110,070	3.0	7.9	7,783
less than 10,000	119,429	3.3	8.5	22,647
Rural Population	2,229,000	61.4	—	—
World Population	3,628,000	100.0	—	—

[a]See Table 2.5 for the sources of this information.
[b]In contrast to Table 2.5, the size categories here are exclusive. They are indicated by listing the lower limit only, since the upper limit is indicated by the lower limit of the next size class. Only the top size category (8 million and over) is an open class. In this table, then, it is possible to add figures and percentages to obtain "collapsed classes," for example, 1 million to 8 million.
Source: Golden, H.H., *Urbanization and Cities.* Lexington, Mass.: D.C. Heath. Table 4.2.
Adapted from Kingsley Davis, *World Urbanization, 1950-1970,* University of California, Berkeley: Institute of International Studies, 1972.

Figure 2.6   Urbanization Levels and Number of Cities in Major Areas and Regions, 1970

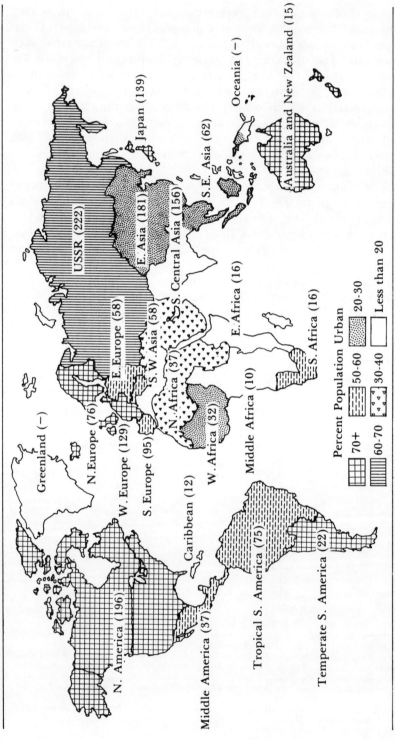

Greenland (–)

N.Europe (76)

W. Europe (129)

S. Europe (95)

Caribbean (12)

W. Africa (32)

Middle Africa (10)

Tropical S. America (75)

Temperate S. America (22)

N. America (196)

Middle America (37)

USSR (222)

E.Europe (58)

S.W. Asia (58)

N.Africa (37)

E. Asia (181)

S. Central Asia (156)

S. Africa (16)

E.Africa (16)

Japan (139)

S.E. Asia (62)

Oceania (–)

Australia and New Zealand (15)

Percent Population Urban

70+

60-70

50-60

30-40

20-30

Less than 20

Source: H.H. Golden, *Urbanization and Cities*, Lexington, Mass.: D.C. Heath, 1981. Figure 4.2a. Based on data from Kingsley Davis, *World Urbanization 1950-1970*, Vol. I (Revised Ed.; University of California, Berkeley: Institute of International Studies, 1970), Table B, pp. 85-111; and Vol. II (ibid., 1972), p. 191.

The inordinate strain that this migration is putting on Latin American cities is best demonstrated by the ubiquitous "favelas" or "barrios" (i.e. slums) surrounding every major city. These contain large concentrations of populations who have poor sanitation, poor housing, and bleak employment prospects.

In the world context, Canada is highly urbanized but the absolute number of people living in Canadian cities is low when compared to other countries. The growth of the Canadian population is also projected to be low relative to these countries (see Figure 2.7). A major megalopolis of 5 million people may not be experienced in Canada for a number of years. With only two cities exceeding 2 million, the problems of urban sprawl, congestion, and inadequate resources have not compounded to the degree experienced in many other societies around the world.

Figure 2.7 Population Trends and Forecasts, Canada and Selected Countries: 1920-2000

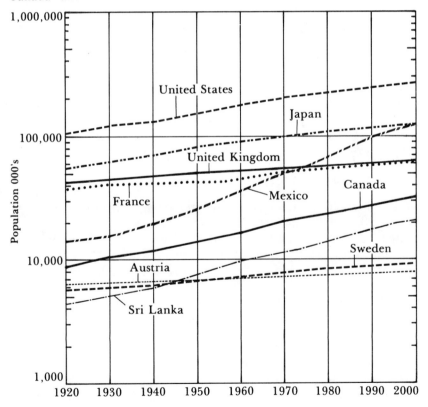

Source: United Nations, *World Population Prospects as Assessed in 1973*, New York: United Nations, 1973, (United Nations publication, Sales No. E. 76. xiii. 4). Table 28, Medium Variant.

The problems that are facing Canadian cities today revolve around the forces of internal migration, from city to city. In the last five years, the growth rates of Alberta cities have been very high (approximately 4.5 percent a year in Calgary and 3.3 percent in Edmonton). This growth is mainly attributable to the movement of people to the West in search of employment. The impact that this movement has had on these cities has included pressure for housing, increased social problems, and increased demands for expensive municipal services (such as police and recreation facilities). While there is a belief that there are positive factors attached to growth, the negative issues must be addressed as well. The recent migration patterns remind us that we are not living in a stagnant urban system, just because we are a heavily urbanized country. The patterns of migration and changes in demographic patterns of fertility and mortality still have important impacts on our urban structure.

Settlement patterns in cities which result from this rapid urbanization are of interest to researchers studying the effects of rural-urban migration and immigration on urban structure. Now that we have dealt with the origins of cities and the changes that have taken place through the population shifts that have led to urbanization, we can turn our attention to the social effects of this movement, i.e. the transformation in society that has resulted in "urbanism as a way of life." This transformation has been viewed in a number of ways. Most often it has been studied in terms of comparisons from one sort of settlement to another. These comparisons include pre-industrial versus industrial cities; rural versus urban areas; and urban versus suburban settings. The following chapter will examine these comparisons.

F. SUMMARY AND CONCLUSIONS

Cities emerged as a result of changes in agricultural technology which allowed for the creation of food surpluses. These surpluses rested in the hands of a few who used them to negotiate for political and military power. The cities that emerged from this concentration of power cultivated writing and the arts. They also promoted a form of social stratification. Trade and commerce centred on the city. The appearance of urban areas, then, related to (1) the evolution of technology, (2) the development of social organization to manage agricultural surpluses and to legitimize existing authority, (3) the importation of skills and goods to a central area, and (4) the development of physical structures giving body to social structure.

Canadian urban development reflects the different bases for the location and growth of cities. The movement from staple trade to agriculture and then to industrialization slowly promoted a national urban system. Today we find that three out of four Canadians live in cities.

Cities have grown as a result of three demographic factors. These include natural increase, migration, and reclassification. The most important of these factors bringing about sustained growth of Canadian cities has been migration (including immigration).

When compared to other countries in the world, Canada is much more urbanized (up to four times as much). At the same time, many countries in the Third World have experienced rapid urban growth in recent years resulting from rural-urban migration and high levels of natural increase in cities. The absolute numbers of people living in these cities are very high. This trend will continue upward in the next few years as these countries experience population growth and increased pressure to occupy and annex rural land.

3 The Urban Transformation

One way in which we can examine how factors in cities promote change is to chart the major structural changes that have taken place in urban settlements over the centuries. Our comparisons here will focus on preindustrial and industrial cities, urban and rural areas, cities and suburbs, and more recent moves back to the country. We can begin by examining the differences of life in pre-industrial and industrial cities.

A. PREINDUSTRIAL VERSUS INDUSTRIAL CITIES

Preindustrial Cities

The ten factors which Childe (1970) argued accompanied the development of the early cities led, as well, to a new social order. Peasant societies evolved into a feudal order. Unlike the folk society, the feudal order had a well-defined and rigid class structure. There was a clear-cut division of labour according to age, sex, and occupation. In all instances, feudal societies contained cities. In these cities resided the political, educational, and religious elite and those who served them. These included craftsmen, servants, and the military. However, these societies, while containing cities, remained predominantly rural.

As Sjoberg (1960:80) states, preindustrial cities tended to be much smaller than their industrial counterparts. Few of them grew larger than 100,000 inhabitants. Their rate of population growth was slow.

In terms of spatial arrangements, the centre of the city acted as the hub of governmental and religious activity more than as a focus of commercial enterprise. This area was the location of elite residences, as well. The lower class and outcaste groups tended to be distributed outwards towards the city boundaries. In addition to the

44

strong segregation based on social class, Sjoberg (1960:98) observes that the land uses in the preindustrial cities also conformed to occupational and ethnic distinctions. These "ghettos" tended to be self-sufficient entities allowing the groups to live socially and physically separate from the rest of the community. Despite this segregation, a minimum of specialization actually existed in land use. A site frequently had a mix of purposes where it was used for religious, educational, and business purposes. For example, religious buildings functioned concurrently as schools. Also, markets were often set up on the grounds of these buildings.

The physical structure of the preindustrial city coincided with a rigidly enforced class structure. One was born into a particular social stratum, and had then to live out life according to the rights and obligations of this position. As Sjoberg (1960:137) emphasizes, the social mobility evident in industrial cities was negligible or non-existent in preindustrial cities. The preindustrial urbanite functioned within a family system. The family became, as a result, the key socializing agent in the community. It also acted as the focus of leisure activity.

The production of goods and services, by means of simple technology, relied on the energy of humans and animals. The division of labour, complex by folk society standards, was very simple. However, while specialization within crafts was minimal, there was widespread specialization according to product. This was evident with the spread of craft guilds. They promoted and regulated the production of specific products, such as gold and silver articles, or cloth. The exclusive nature of guilds made them even more powerful, both economically and politically. This was especially true in Europe in the Middle Ages. A remnant of the former importance of these guilds can be seen in the impressive Grande Place in Belgium. The guild halls covered with gold leaf have pride of place as they surround the main square of the old city.

The political structure in these cities was controlled by a chosen few. They administered according to the feudal rules of order wherein loyalty was pledged to the elite in return for protection from spiritual, as well as animate, enemies. Sjoberg (1960:141) places special emphasis on the importance of ascription (birth) in deciding who was selected into all positions in the government bureaucracy springing up to govern these cities. This is one area where the preindustrial city differed markedly from industrial cities. In the latter, achievement and skills are the criteria normally used to decide who takes part in leadership and where the social status will be allocated.

These differences in city types are illustrated by research done by Katz (1969:211) on the social structure of Hamilton in the 1850s. Katz found that the preindustrial city was very much segmented by differences in wealth distribution. At that time, nearly half of the assessed wealth in the city was in the hands of a mere 5 percent of the work force, or 125 people. At the other end of the spectrum, the bottom 20 percent, or roughly the poorest 500 people, had only 1.6 percent of the wealth. With industrialization, there is an expectation that this wealth becomes more generally distributed. This accompanies an increase in social and economic stratification due to the advent of white-collar managerial positions. However, the lot of the poor is not always improved. As a city such as Hamilton continued to grow, the increased social stratification brought about by industrialization and the formation of an industrial working class increased the odds against lower-class children or adults improving their social position. At the time of early industrialization in Hamilton, cultural patterns associated with family size and school attendance retarded the chances of social mobility.

Industrial Cities

The industrial-urban society, in contrast to the feudal order, uses inanimate sources of energy and scientific applications to the production of goods and services. This advanced technology requires skills to operate. The class system therefore emphasizes achievement (based on education) rather than ascription. Social power is diffused throughout the society. Geographical and social mobility create competition for space and resources in cities. Cities become the central focus of the society. The majority of the population live in or near these settlements.

As cities developed, there was more universal access to educational institutions. Skilled labour was in greater demand. Wealth became more widely dispersed. The working class, through unionization, became more politicized. These factors promoted stronger emphasis on achievement criteria in hiring and in the development of social groupings. With urbanization came changes in the social structure. There was a movement away from family status to achieved status. Education and learning became the passport to social mobility. The increased opportunities for this learning and the chances of getting work in industry attracted many people to the cities where this industry located. In cities such as Hamilton, going through the early stages of this development, the transition came slowly. The means of training and education were not always available and not always used. The traditional values held sway over the behaviour of the individual during the time of change.

A concomitant effect of industrial urbanization is the very strong differentiation of the population according to income, occupation, ethnic, religious, and spatial characteristics. It has been argued, in fact, that the need for an administrative and political apparatus to operate the industrial order helped encourage the development of cities (Weber, 1958). This argument has been expanded further to point out that cities came to be formed from the need to consolidate economic and political structures within industrial society (Sjoberg, 1960). In his famous study, *French Canada in Transition,* Everett Hughes (1943) describes the change that took place in Cantonville, Québec as a result of industrialization. In 1911, Cantonville was a country trading town with a population (including the rural township) of 2,605. By 1937, the town had grown from a rural service community to an industrialized community of 19,424. Industry by this time employed 4,600 people and produced products for the national Canadian market (Hughes, 1943:29). The newcomers to the town were predominantly French-Canadian rural folk who left unproductive farms to seek work in the industrializing town. There was some influx of English migrants. However, as Hughes (1943:31) points out, the English arrived in the town to perform new and specialized functions. They held all of the positions of authority and advanced technical training in the local industries. At the same time, the French constituted the majority of people employed in industry. Local industries and service enterprises were generally owned, as well, by French Canadians.

In Cantonville, the early stages of industrialization combined achievement and ascription with the best jobs in the industries being populated by English engineers and managers. There were distinctions in the French-speaking community, as well. The non-industrial sector was controlled by family interests. Of interest is the finding that the government in Cantonville was almost exclusively controlled by French Canadians.

Over the years, the transition from a traditional to industrial society combined the new values of technical advancement with the old traditions of the importance of family and religion. The tension between these values led to friction between the ethnic groups in Cantonville who identified differently with the new, as opposed to the traditional, ways.

With people moving to industrial cities, then, we find a dramatic change in the nature of social differentiation in society. We find political power redistributed from rural to urban areas. We find economic strength centred in cities with a shift in patterns of living to conform to the constraints and opportunities of urban settings. The separation of individuals' homes from their place of work; the need for services to cater to a densely populated and heterogeneous population; the requirement for social control agencies to maintain order; and the legitimization for the allocation of resources all had to be developed to cater to the needs of this population.

A number of negative factors have been identified as consequences of rapid urbanization. Increased opportunities for work accompanied breakdown in family ties. Many people saw this as an indicator of the loss of important rural values with the coming of mass urbanization. (This will be discussed in the next section.) Also, the large influx of people into urban areas brought about staggering demands for housing. The housing that was provided in early industrial cities proved to be the breeding ground of disease and crime. Inadequate sanitary facilities, poor police protection, and limited fire safety led to desperate housing conditions in many of these early industrial cities. While the more serious environmental conditions have been cleaned up with the introduction of sewers and local health boards, many industrial cities today continue to have problems which are a function of their size and a lack of resources to meet the needs of their inhabitants.

B. THE RURAL-URBAN CONTINUUM

There is another comparison that is useful to us in understanding the nature of urban life. It has been widely argued in the urban literature that the movement towards cities has been especially traumatic for people who were closely constrained by the traditional values of rural society. The inability to cope with many different stimuli from strange surroundings and the disappearance of external control from community leaders contributed to social disorganization and individual alienation.

In an influential article originally written in 1938, Louis Wirth (1938:11) argued that the continued growth of American cities led to an increasing mixture of diverse ethnic, occupational, and income groups in densely settled areas. These factors combined to create social environments where there was loneliness, alienation, and social deviance. Wirth argued that especially for migrants who came from rural areas and small towns, the move to the city could destroy close family ties and could lead to aimlessness and unhappiness. The rural-ruban continuum was conceived as a way of distinguishing, in socio-cultural terms, life in cities from life elsewhere.

As Redfield (1953) points out, civilization occurs when a community is no longer small, isolated, homogeneous, and self-sufficient. The division of labour is no longer simple. Impersonal relations take the place of personal relations. Familial connections are modified or supplanted by political ties and economic contract. Thinking becomes reflective and systematic (Redfield, 1953:22). This remaking of man, according to Redfield, is the work of the city. The folk societies have been transformed by contact with urban influences. The mobility of people away from the rural environments into cities has made this contrast even more striking. Based on the opinion of Wirth (1938), that major variations in numbers and density of human groupings bring about significant changes in the nature of social relationships, five major differences between rural and urban communities have been identified (Poplin, 1979).

First, the urbanite enjoys greater anonymity than the ruralite. In order to gain the freedom from scrutiny of family and neighbours enjoyed by the urbanite, rural dwellers have to leave their hamlet, village, or town. Of course, the urbanites may have to pay the cost for this anonymity in loneliness or lack of social support. Some contrary evidence to this has been produced by those who have found strong and viable ethnic enclaves for immigrants from rural societies in inner cities. These groups maintain tight control over individuals and provide strong mutual support. A study done in Montreal, in fact, demonstrated that ethnic communities were very much self-contained. They developed their own institutions to cope with the host society (Breton, 1968).

Second, differences exist in the occupational structure of rural and urban communities, with urban areas characterized by a greater division of labour. Industrial employment and work in service industries create many different occupations not found in a predominantly agricultural, rural society. This occupational variation is reflected in the development of a complex status hierarchy in urban societies. This is not evident in predominantly rural societies where the status differences are few but distinct.

Third, urban areas tend to be much more heterogeneous than rural communities. A large percentage of the population of a small rural community may belong to the same political party. They may attend the same church. Also, they may share the same ethnic background. Alternatively, the population of a city is composed of people of all types and of widely differing outlooks on life (Poplin, 1979:34).

Fourth, in contrast to rural areas, impersonal and formally prescribed relationships are likely to flourish in the urban setting. It is impossible to develop primary relations with all people with whom one comes into contact. At the same time, people in rural areas may know most of the people with whom they associate. Even when they do run across strangers, ruralites may freely interact with them or offer them assistance (Poplin, 1979:34).

Finally, in cities people frequently judge others' status based on the neighbourhoods in which they live, the type of cars they drive, and the types of clothes that they wear. In rural communities, on the other hand, people tend to know each other. Therefore, they are able to judge, rank, and evaluate others on the basis of their personal characteristics.

These distinctions between rural and urban life are well illustrated in the study done by Burnet (1978) of the Hanna area in Alberta in the 1930s. As she describes it, with town growth, differences developed between the rural and urban people. Economically, the presence of the railroad allowed the town to function separately from the farm communities. Socially, the townspeople began to develop organizations, such as churches, lodges, and schools, without the aid and support of the rural people. This reduced the social contacts with the farmers and increased the differentiation between rural and urban ways of life.

Further, a mobile young male group settled in the town. This group owed no loyalty to the old time order. There developed, then, a casual attitude towards strangers which was not present in the town before. Other more visible distinctions developed between rural and town people. The townsman could be distinguished from the farmer at a glance. "The farmer wears durable, drab, and loose-fitting work clothes and clumsy, dark and usually unfashionable 'good clothes' which contrast strongly with the business suits or sport suits of the business and professional men . . ." (Burnet, 1978:89). As suggested by Poplin, the greater anonymity of the town coupled with people of different occupational, social, and political backgrounds created more impersonal relations. Unlike the rural environment, it promoted the use of material objects to assess status and rank.

In the early days of urban development in this country, then, the distinctions of rural and urban ways of life grew to cause major divisions in economic, political, and social structures of the society. However, these rural-urban distinctions are less evident in contemporary times. This is true because communication and transportation networks have tied urban and rural areas more closely together. Many of the attributes of urban living can now be found in rural settlements (Dewey, 1960). Gans (1970:71) has argued that the simple rural-urban distinction overlooks the diversity of life styles found in urban areas. He feels that a more useful distinction can be drawn between the life styles of sub-groups within the contemporary city rather than relying on the assumption that rural versus urban location creates natural differences in the ways in which people live. This view of urbanism led to studies that examined the evolution of differences in the ways in which city dwellers live. The most obvious comparison to be made focussed on the development of suburbs.

C. SUBURBANIZATION

Suburban Development

Suburban development on a grand scale came about in the 1950s. It occurred through the combined effects of large natural increase in the population (with the "baby boom"), immigration, and migration to the city from rural areas. These led to a spillover of urban populations into the surrounding countryside. The need was expressed for a large number of single-family houses to give shelter to the many newly formed households. With this came the demand for environments that would be suitable for raising children away from the congestion and dangers of inner-city neighbourhoods. As a consequence, large tracts of suburban development appeared on the Canadian landscape. Large-scale suburban growth led in many cities towards uniformity of housing and, it was believed, a uniformity of life style in these outlying areas.

Recent trends in suburbanization indicate that there is a continuing drop in numbers of people living in the Canadian inner cities (see Table 3.1). From 1971 to 1976, Montreal showed the greatest decline with a loss of 133,806 persons, Toronto lost 79,468 and Vancouver decreased by 16,110. As we pointed out in Chapter 2, this loss of inner-city residents is balanced by an increased proportion of urban populations living in the remainder of the urban core and the fringe areas.

Table 3.1.
Population Change of Nine Central Cities, 1971-1976

Central city	Numerical change	Percentage change
Montréal	−133,806	−11.0
Toronto	−79,468	−11.1
Vancouver	−16,110	−3.8
Québec	−10,751	−5.7
Windsor	−6,774	−3.3
Halifax	−4,153	−3.4
Saint John	−3,083	−3.5
Sudbury	−2,842	−2.8
St. John's	−1,838	−2.1

Source: 1976 Census of Canada, Catalogue 92-806, Table 6. Cited in Statistics Canada, *Canada's Cities.* Ottawa: Statistics Canada, Table 4.
Reproduced by permission of the Minister of Supply and Services Canada.

The Suburban Myth

The major move to the suburbs did not occur without a great deal of comment about life styles in these areas. The stories that came out of the suburbs characterized them as bland and homogeneous with people living a life dedicated to "keeping up with the Jones's". Berger (1972) describes the "typical" suburb. "Approaching suburbs from the outside, one is immediately struck by rows of new 'ranch-type' houses either identical in design or with minor variations built into a basic plan, winding streets, neat lawns, two-car garages, infant trees, and bicycles and tricycles lining the sidewalks.

Nearby is the modern ranch-type school and the even more modern shopping centre dominated by the department store branch or the giant super-market, itself flanked by a pastel-dotted expanse of a parking lot." (Berger, 1972: 6).

The "myth of suburbia" was that living in a tract suburb was temporary. Its residents were upwardly mobile. They lived there only until a promotion or a company transfer permitted or required them to purchase a more opulent home. According to the myth, a new type of hyperactive social life developed in the suburbs. The rich organizational structure that developed was promoted by the homogeneity of suburbanites. They generally came from the same backgrounds and shared the same interests. They were seen as escapees from the rigours of city life. They came in search of environments where they could raise their children and pursue their hobbies in peace.

Riesman (1958) cast a new light on the suburban myth when he characterized suburbs as places of "sadness," where people found little or no social contact. This impression runs counter to the view of suburbs as locations of high social contact. Demands for conformity, according to Riesman, removed any chance for people to develop unique personalities. The emphasis on not breaking the norms of the community was very strong. Loneliness and alienation were seen to develop among the people (especially the women) who lived in these areas. The fact that many different life-style groups and many different class groups found their way to the suburbs did not do much to reduce the negative views that many people had about them.

The myth of suburbs is very much a product of people's impressions of white-collar suburbs. It ignores differences in the types of economic and family groups who end up living in these environments — a point we will pursue later in the book. The different perspectives to be discussed in the following chapters will focus on the various ways in which researchers have come to grips with the suburban myth and the role that suburbs play in the overall urban way of life.

D. POPULATION TURNAROUND

Demographic Change and the Back-to-the-Country Movement

We referred in Chapter 2 to the recent demographic change that has taken place in Canada with the movement of people away from the urban areas and into rural areas. The importance of this migration rests with the fact that a major investment of time and money will be spent in providing facilities for former urban dwellers who now reside in non-metropolitan areas. In addition, many of these people will live in these areas but still work in the cities. This will create an even greater burden on cities to meet the rising costs of providing services.

Long (1980) lists four reasons for the migration of people back to the countryside. First, there is a continued trend to decentralization of employment. This is made possible by the improvement of transportation and communication networks. People are drawn away from metropolitan areas, as a result. The growth of the service industries in these newly populated areas also attracts people.

Second, non-metropolitan areas have become the locations for a renewed search for energy. The growth of coal-mining regions and areas of oil and gas extraction provides employment attractions to people from all over the country.

Third, non-metropolitan areas have attracted people who have retired, and those who are looking for recreational opportunities not available in the cities. More people are retiring at an earlier age. With life expectancy increasing, the result is an increase in active years which can be spent away from the metropolitan employment centres in scenic and amenity-rich locations.

Fourth, there is a clear preference among many urban residents for living in small towns and rural areas. This leads them to seek out opportunities to act on such preferences. There is a recurrent suggestion that people will take cuts in real income in order to realize non-metropolitan living preferences (Long, 1980:70).

Overall, these four factors suggest that a heterogeneous group of movers consisting of older persons (retirees), young wage-earners, and middle-aged persons, who may be quite willing to sacrifice income and careers, is making its way to the countryside.

Migration is a reflection of basic social change. As Bogue (1959) points out, the attraction of newcomers to an area may be brought about by the improved occupational opportunities afforded by resource development or through government decentralization. The consequences for the small communities of the rapid influx of these migrants into the area can be dramatic both in social and in economic terms.

An important finding reported by McVey (1978) is that new migrants (including immigrants) into smaller rural communities in Canada tend to be very different from the long-term residents in terms of socio-economic status and family size. The in-migrant groups tend to have smaller families. They also are more likely to belong to professional and managerial occupation groups than are the non-migrants. The problems of friction that may develop between dissimilar groups in their expectations of what the town can and should offer to meet their needs will grow increasingly pressing as this migration speeds up.

In communities surrounding the major urban centres, the consequences of the population turnaround do lead to tensions. Providing adequate servicing to the different life-cycle groups making their way to these areas poses serious difficulties. Many of these satellite, non-metropolitan towns are gaining large growth in population because of the cheaper housing available outside of the city limits. In the Edmonton region, the small towns have grown at a rate of up to 10 percent each year since 1975. What this growth does, rather than pit long-term residents against short-term residents, is put life-cycle groups up against one another.

Leduc, 15 miles south of Edmonton, began as a service town for the surrounding farm communities and grew as a result of farmers retiring off the farm. When the international airport was built there, it became a convenient area for people who had to travel for their work to locate their families. In more recent years, this town has become a popular place for Edmontonians to find cheap housing. The attraction of different types of people to this area, ranging from the retired couples off the farm to the young family with children and the young singles locating near the airport, leads to differences in demands from the community. This is especially evident in their attitudes towards growth of the town. The older people want the town to stay the same size. The women with children want it to grow so they can have access to better services. The concern about the maintenance of small town values is especially strong among the older people. They see the large amount of growth leading to a possible deterioration of their quality of life in this area.

Hodge and Qadeer (1980) pursue this with findings from national data. They state that the 1971 population of 1,486 small towns (less than 10,000 people) was 2,229,000. This increased by 141,000 in the five years up to 1976 or 6.3 percent. They go on to point out that this buoyancy of town population is striking when compared to population growth rates for other major settlement types in Canada for the two most recent five-year census periods (see Table 3.2). While urban growth rates dropped (from 13.5 percent to 6.7 percent for metropolitan areas), the growth of towns stayed pretty constant. Some of that growth is likely to be attributable to movement into these areas from cities.

In smaller rural communities, the dilemma of providing costly services to people in search of cheaper homes in non-congested areas is posing a serious problem, as well. Sinclair and Westhues (1974) have shown that the pressures from new migrants can have major implications on how the physical design and preservation of natural areas in a rural area are developed. In their description of "Fringe-town," Ontario they describe the major battles that developed over the construction of the village's first apartment buildings and the

Table 3.2.
Comparative Population Growth Rates for Major Settlement Types, Canada,
1966-1971 and 1971-1976

Settlement type	5-year population growth rate (%)	
	1966-1971	1971-1976
All urban	11.4	5.8
Metropolitan areas[a]	13.5	6.7
Rural farm	−25.8	−27.1
Rural nonfarm	10.8	22.8
Small town (Inc.)[b]	6.6	6.3
Canada	7.8	6.6

[a] Those identified in 1976 Census.
[b] Incorporated centres under 10,000 population only.
Source: Hodge, G. and M.A. Qadeer, 1980. "The Persistence of Canadian Towns and
Villages: Small is Viable" from *Urban Geography*, 1980, Volume 1, page 346 by permission
of V.H. Winston & Sons, Silver Spring, Maryland.

construction of a bridge over the village's area of natural beauty —
its gorge on the river.

The views of oldtimers who saw economic benefits from growth
came into conflict with newcomers who felt the town should retain
its small-town atmosphere. Many of the latter were using the village
as a suburb of Toronto — commuting regularly to the city. This
group wanted to retain the historical value of the area. But their
very presence contributed to growth and to demands for expanded
services. The character of the village, as well as its social and
economic structure, was threatened by the urbanizing influence of
its proximity to a growing metropolis. The implications of this turnaround will only be truly understood in the years to come.

We have witnessed just such a condition in the rapid growth of
Fort McMurray, an Alberta boom town, which drew thousands of
people to work the oil sands. The problems of crime and social
breakdown were not evident in the town prior to the boom. But with
the stress of the jobs and the displacement felt by many people in
having to move to this area, which was less than prepared to handle
this rapid growth, many types of social breakdown occurred.

Gartrell, et al. (1980) found that Fort McMurray had experienced rapid population growth, multiplying 20 times over 20 years.
It contains a high proportion of males and experiences high population turnover. Only 7 percent of the population in 1980 was 45 and
over. The labour force is highly mobile, with many people having
relatively unstable employment histories.

In terms of life in the community, people express dissatisfaction
with social life and freedom from crime and vandalism. At the same
time, the community is viewed as being dynamic with good employ-

ment opportunities. The factors that attracted people to Fort McMurray are appreciated. The crush of new arrivals inevitably leads, at the same time, to the creation of social and physical problems. The challenge of Canadian frontier development involves anticipating the difficulties connected with servicing large numbers of people in resource towns and diminishing the effects of unstable economic conditions on the social conditions in these environments.

Non-farm Rural Settlement

The back-to-the-country movement is impacting on rural areas as much as it is on small towns, although the effects are somewhat different. The growth of acreage developments has led to a form of sprawl on the urban fringe, much of this occurring on prime agricultural areas. At the end of 1974, in the Calgary area, 83,000 acres had been subdivided for acreage parcels of 45 acres in size. Another 60,000 acres will be subdivided for parcels 24 acres in size. Of this land, 62 percent is classified as prime agricultural (Spear, 1979:31).

The reasons people gave for moving to acreages in the Calgary region included the desire for privacy, better environments for children, a preference for rural living, and a desire to escape the city. These same people, for the most part, commuted long distances into Calgary for work, social visits, and entertainment. The desire for rural life goes hand in hand with accessibility to urban services and employment, at least when looking at acreage dwellers.

E. THE BACK-TO-THE-CITY MOVEMENT

Gentrification of Inner-City Neighbourhoods

At the same time as the movement into the rural areas is happening, there appears to be a similar movement back into the inner cities (although the net migration flow is still outward). Evidence of this new desirability of the inner city is the revitalization of dilapidated neighbourhoods by young, professional couples. This "gentrification" or "white-painting" has been especially evident in areas that were originally seen as lower-income. The displacement of low- income residents has created some concern. The price of renovated housing in these older neighbourhoods removes it as an affordable alternative to former residents. In defence of this inner city revitalization is the fact that older neighbourhoods are being saved by the investment people are willing to make to assure their survival. We will examine the debates surrounding "urban renewal" in greater detail in Chapter 6.

Who are the new migrants moving into these areas? Initial speculation in the United States was that the revival was due to the movement of suburban residents back into the city. In fact, as we indicated above, cities have continued to lose people in the early family life cycle to the suburbs. What appears to be occurring is that some people populating these older neighbourhoods have lived somewhere else in the inner city before moving to their new home. In a study done in Edmonton, the 1978 Edmonton Area Study, of those people currently living in the inner city area, 48 percent had lived in some other part of the inner city before moving to their current address; 33 percent had lived in the suburbs; and 17 percent moved in from out of town (Kennedy, et al., 1978).

From research done in Winnipeg's inner city (*Urban Forum*, June, 1977), some interesting findings about the reasons for living downtown were produced. The study found that people living in the inner city were generally of varied ethnic origin. They had lower income and education levels compared to the rest of the city's inhabitants. The proportions of single-parent families, senior citizens, and immigrant groups were also higher than the city averages. The residential mobility of this group was higher than elsewhere in the city. At the same time, nearly a third had lived at the same address for over 10 years. Most people interviewed (70 percent) lived in rented dwellings (*Urban Forum*, 1977:8).

People living in the inner city stated that they mostly liked the convenience of central city living, which provided access to the major facilities in the downtown area. They said they liked the other people living in the neighbourhood. The cost of living was lower, and there was good quality housing and quiet surroundings. The residents also felt the area was safe from crime. These characteristics are often not associated with inner-city living. Yet, the convenience of location combined with quiet neighbourhoods can make the inner city a very desirable place to live.

Revitalization and Redevelopment

The revitalization of places like Cabbagetown in Toronto, Strathcona in Edmonton, and Point Grey in Winnipeg is part of a new trend in urban development. This will probably be further encouraged in future years by the increasing cost of gasoline, making the trip from distant suburbs into downtown offices increasingly expensive. The importance of this movement for the boost that it gives to the financial resources of the city must also be underlined. It is a positive portent of healthy cities in the future. The desire to gamble on the revival of older neighbourhoods provides a city with people who have a strong investment in seeing that it succeeds in terms of services, security, and community.

Redevelopment is taking place in the form of multiple dwellings as well. In Vancouver, since the early 1950s, some 50 percent of all new apartments have been located in the West End. This area, approximately one mile square, is bordered by the downtown commercial core, the harbour, the beaches of English Bay and Stanley Park. Its proximity to the beaches and to the downtown made this area most desirable to multiple dwelling development. The apartments that were built attracted both young people setting up their first home and older people who could no longer maintain their own houses. What is interesting to note in this movement from single family to multiple dwellings is that most of the people were already living in the inner-city area (Gaylor, 1973:203). These changes in the character of inner cities are leading to the development of more compact cities. Also, the preservation of old neighbourhoods and the enhancement of historical resources attracts the capital needed to revitalize inner-core areas.

The dichotomy that exists between back-to-the-city and back-to-the-country moves serves as an interesting point of comparison for future cities. Will there be greater momentum towards decentralization of cities or will they become even more compact? Planners will have to cope with this question in the future.

F. SUMMARY AND CONCLUSIONS

The urban transformation has taken on a number of different characteristics over the years. With industrialization, the cities that developed in predominantly rural preindustrial societies took on more importance. They grew to become the central settlement place of most people in these societies. Industrial cities reflect changes in the social structure of the society as preindustrial cities had done before them. There is great social and geographical mobility in industrial cities. Work places are separated from home. The households focus on the nuclear rather than the extended family. The city becomes the centre of the political and economic life of the society.

Cities have been transformed by migration from rural areas in preindustrial and industrial times. The forces of industrialization have been most powerful, however, in drawing people out of rural areas and into the cities. This movement has brought out the contrasts that exist between rural and urban life. Poplin (1979:33-34) summarizes these differences. First, the urbanite enjoys greater anonymity than the ruralite. Second, differences exist in the occupational structure of rural and urban areas. Third, urban areas are more socially heterogeneous than rural communities. Fourth, impersonal relationships are more likely to appear in urban than in rural areas. Fifth, in cities people are judged on their possessions rather than their personal characteristics. In early days, these contrasts were very strong. With the continued urbanization of society, these differences are becoming less significant.

Another factor contributing to the urban transformation has been the move to suburbs. This move occurred for people forming families looking for good environments to raise children. The myths that grew up around life in suburbs portrayed them as places of uniformity and intense interaction. This myth was shattered by researchers who characterized suburbs as places of great loneliness and sadness for many residents. These contrasting views have been attributed to the fact that suburbs are not in fact homogeneous but consist of people from many different backgrounds.

Two more recent trends that have been identified in cities are population turnaround and a back-to-the-city movement. Population turnaround involves a revitalization of rural non-farm areas by people leaving cities. This is prompted by a desire for small-town or rural life styles. This movement has led to a number of changes taking place in small communities trying to cope with this new growth and the demands that the new residents bring with them. It has also raised concerns for those who feel that the growth taking place in rural areas through acreage development is taking good farm land out of production.

The back-to-the-city movement has involved people who are already residents of the inner city staying in the downtown areas to renovate existing housing. Alternatively, they are attracted by new housing developments. The proximity of the downtown amenities and work has made this type of settlement pattern increasingly more popular. As a result, there have been some positive effects in the revitalization of inner-city neighbourhoods. The negative effects have been felt most by lower-income people who lose cheaper housing in the inner city because of this redevelopment.

In the following chapters, the forces of urban transformation will be examined in the context of the impacts that they have on cities. This analysis will contrast competition, choice, and allocation as factors in this transformation process.

4 Human Ecology and Competition

A. THE ORIGINS OF THE THEORY OF HUMAN ECOLOGY

The leading figure in the development of the ecological perspective of urban change was the sociologist Robert Ezra Park. The scene of his research was Chicago in the 1920s and 1930s. At the time of Park's research, Chicago was undergoing rapid change and growth through the influx of large numbers of immigrants from Europe. Park (1925:22) observed that the changes the city was experiencing gave the urban researcher the opportunity to study human behaviour in a large natural laboratory where a wide variety of factors affected it.

Park (1925:1) sees the city as more than simply a structure containing individuals, services, and institutions providing certain support functions. The city, to Park, is a state of mind. It is also a body of customs, traditions, and attitudes. It is not, from Park's point of view, merely a physical mechanism and an artificial construction. He sees the city as a product of nature and, particularly, human nature. This human nature is transmitted through media, transportation, and education. The city is the product, then, of the complex interaction of human cultures and ideas.

Basic to Park's perspective is the idea of order. In his mind, the evolution of cities comes from the interaction of both physical organization and moral order. The physical organization is based on ecological and economic determinants of the structure of the city. The moral order is based on what Park refers to as the influences of sympathy, rivalry, and economic necessity. Underlying all three of these concepts is the idea of competition. Within the moral order, this competition could centre around ethnicity, economic status, family status, or race. Competition is driven by the size, concentration, and distribution of the population in the city. Based on the ability to compete, which varies by income, different groups are able to claim better locations, better access to services, and better quality environments (Park, 1925:12-23).

Park seeks to better explain the way in which these forces of competition influence the development of cities. He argues that the city evolved and changed much in the same way as the biologist views changes in the ecological balance of plants and animals in the natural environment. When using this analogy, what becomes of central importance in the work of Park and his colleagues is the process of change, not the change itself (Park, 1925:2).

As McKenzie (1926) describes it, geography is concerned with place, ecology with process. Location, as a geographical concept, signifies position on the earth's surface. Location, as an ecological concept, signifies position in a spatial grouping of interacting human beings. Ecological distribution is then the spatial distribution of human beings and human activities resulting from the interplay of social and economic forces. The ecologists saw the evolution of social order in cities resulting from the relationship that people had to the environment and to one another (McKenzie, 1926). As Hawley (1981:432) puts it, ecology studies the interaction of population with environment. The effect of this interaction is adaptation. The focus of ecology is on the total population rather than the individual as the unit of observation. It views causal forces of change as impersonal rather than personal. Norms of behaviour are defined as regularities in organization. They are seen as products of these impersonal forces rather than causes of them. People do not regulate the city and city change, rather it regulates them (Hawley, 1981).

B. NATURAL AREAS AND NEIGHBOURHOODS

Natural Areas

In drawing from the biological analogy, Park talks about the evolution of natural areas. These are areas of common ground where people who share certain like backgrounds and traditions cluster. These areas form because of the cohesive forces of community and the exclusive forces of segregation.

The most obvious manifestation of this clustering of people is the formation of neighbourhoods. The neighbourhood is the most basic social unit in the city. The ecologists see it forming as a result of the natural processes of competition. The neighbourhood fosters community attachment and local sentiment. It is also viewed as a basic political unit, although it survives without the benefit of formal organization. Neighbourhood in the minds of the ecologists appears to equate with community. There is a certain level of social interaction, common background, and shared purpose. It is in the neighbourhood that individuals receive social and economic support. Through the neighbourhood individuals are able to make changes in their life style consistent with changes in the urban environment.

The concept of neighbourhood will be used throughout this book in different ways according to the perspectives being studied. The idea of neighbourhood is important as it allows us to combine the social and physical aspects of city life into one concept which has spatial and social significance. As the ecologists use this term, it relates to the identification of people with like backgrounds who gather in areas of the city that suit their needs and their life styles. It allows the ecologists to outline spatially the processes of change taking place in cities. It also corresponds to the way in which the people themselves identify their living spaces. In a study of slum areas in Chicago, Suttles (1972) talks about the territoriality of social groups in these areas, where there is a discernible idea of protecting their own "turf." This turf behaviour is especially evident among the young gang members from the different ethnic groups who fight off all incursions into their territory.

Defining Neighbourhoods

The spatial definition of neighbourhoods has posed some problems for researchers over the years, as there has been increased integration and assimilation of people into the city. The usefulness of neighbourhood as a concept remains, however.

Warren (1977) identifies six major functional roles for neighbourhoods (quoted in Gold, 1982:116). First, a neighbourhood can serve as the arena for social interaction. This is the place in which casual greetings with neighbours help to develop loose networks of social contact and mutual support. The original natural areas, which were defined as homogeneous by the ecologists, were assumed to be the primary source of interaction. These networks develop both because of the proximity of people but also because of the shared interests and activities of people who live near to one another. We can study the underpinnings of this concept of networking further in Chapter 5.

Of concern to the ecologists is the fact that the homogeneity of neighbourhoods leads to shared life styles. Greer (1956) and Bell and Boat (1957) studied neighbourhoods defined in this way. They argue that there are higher levels of social interaction in these areas than where people are different from one another. The ecological formation, it is argued, creates a community.

The second role of the neighbourhood centres around interpersonal influence. Role models are provided for people to raise children or to keep up their property. This combines with the view of

solidarity needed in dealing with municipal authorities over transportation plans or ideas about redevelopment. Often, the political
structure is inadequate in dealing with the concerns of small areas,
which may form only a small part of a ward or service delivery
region. The emergence of neighbourhood-based leaders functions
to provide grass roots responses to community plans and negative
social impacts of city policies. More on this in Chapter 6.

Third, the neighbourhood can be a source of mutual aid. Neighbours are important for babysitting or for day-to-day support for
children. This is coupled with the need for people to be available to
provide surveillance of property to protect it from crime and
vandalism.

Fourth, the neighbourhood can serve as a base for formal and informal groups which serve as integrating agencies to help people
who are new to the area and need assistance adapting. Community
self-help programmes or women's auxiliaries, and "welcome
wagons" are often offered on a neighbourhood basis to provide con-
tinuity in an area and to assist people to find their way around.
Some cities also have recreational facilities operated on a neighbourhood level where they reach the most people.

In Edmonton, community leagues have been formed which
divide the city into 132 areas. These leagues are run by an elected
executive. They offer a wide range of local recreational and social
service programmes in each area with funding support from the
city, as well as money earned through volunteer support. The
responsiveness of these community leagues is increased because of
their ability to be sensitive to the particular needs of the people living in the neighbourhoods serviced by them.

Fifth, the neighbourhood can serve as a reference group. In the
minds of the ecologists it is the need to find people who reinforce the
attitudes and beliefs that they themselves hold, that leads people to
seek out others like them. Aided by the natural process of competition, this search leads to the development of neighbourhoods containing similar people with similar life styles.

Sixth, related to this concern about reference groups is a need to
consider the social status that neighbourhoods confer on their residents. Much of the task involved in finding a new home revolves
around a concern about locating in an area that provides the status
level that people consider appropriate. This status difference can be
fairly accurately worked out in a hierarchical fashion for all neighbourhoods spread throughout the city. The combination of good
housing, good location, and good services allows one area to compare more favourably with another where the quality is not as good.
The reflection of this status on the individual living there provides
important incentives for people to locate in these higher-status

areas. The ecologists argue that the competition for such spaces is a basic process involved in the normal development of the structure of the city.

C. ECOLOGICAL PROCESSES

To the ecologist, the boundaries of these natural areas are not concrete. A great deal of shifting of boundaries and mobility is constantly taking place in the competition for space and resources. This competition manifests itself in the development of areas in the city that evolve according to certain constant processes of change. The processes include "centralization," "decentralization," "concentration," "deconcentration," "segregation," "invasion," and "succession." The overriding process is "competition" (McKenzie, 1926).

Centralization refers to the tendency for selected institutions and services to cluster near the city's focal points of transportation. The central business district (CBD), for example, becomes the focal area of the city's business. Decentralization refers to the tendency to move away from the central focus of the city so that activities and buildings are spread throughout the urban area. Concentration is the massing of people in an area, as in the case of a high-rise development project. Deconcentration is the outward movement from existing clusters. An example of this is the population movement to the suburbs.

Segregation is the tendency for various groups and institutions to locate in separate and distinct parts of the city. Ecologists use the concept of segregation in several ways. First of all, it refers to the tendency for similar ecological units, such as ethnic groups, to cluster near one another. (The forces of discrimination and prejudice which may have led to this segregation are of little interest to the ecologists, however.) Secondly, it is used to highlight the fact that various parts of the city are characterized by different patterns of land use. These include residential, business, and industrial areas. Thirdly, classical ecologists saw segregation as the primary factor leading to the development of "natural areas." Because segregation brings together people who are racially, economically, and socially homogeneous, they also tend to share common interests, bonds, and needs. We see groups with common interests and needs emerging within natural areas.

Invasion refers to a situation in which one group or institution encroaches on the territory held by another group or institution. For example, invasion occurs when the Central Business District (CBD) expands into immediately adjacent areas. The movement of middle-class families into inner-city neighbourhoods to renovate or "gentrify" old houses is also a case of invasion. The arrival of a new immigrant group in a neighbourhood and their gradual pushing out of the resident group is a third example.

Succession refers to the completed process of invasion where an area is completely converted from one use to another. "Succession is temporal as well as territorial. It entails the replacement of old population groups by new ones and the appearance of new and different institutions in a given area. This may require years of continuous and steady change" (Poplin, 1979:94).

Competition sorts out these various groups. The wealthy become isolated from the poor because of their greater ability to command and control choice residential sites. On the other hand, certain minority groups are unable to compete at all. They must, therefore, take up residence in the less desirable sections of the city. Organization of the city is constantly in a state of flux and change.

D. MODELS OF URBAN DEVELOPMENT

Early critics pointed out that although these ecological concepts are useful for describing changes that occur in urban areas, they do not provide hypotheses that can be empirically tested. To overcome this problem some ecologists integrated these concepts into models of ecological development. They then used these models to describe the growth and development of cities. Consistent with the ecological premise that ecology is a process, the models focussed on the forces of expansion in cities. Using the basic processes of change as the underlying variables, the ecologists sought to describe this expansion in terms of fixed patterns of growth and dispersion of population. Basic to this perspective is the concept that cities operate as do any other organisms that seek equilibrium and balance. The new ingredients in the overall urban society, the immigrants, are forced to adapt to change and compete for space and resources. This first brings imbalance and then balance in the structure of the city. As Burgess (1925) argues, differentiation into natural economic and cultural groupings gives form and character to the city. The sorting process whereby groups are segregated and dispersed through the urban area is based on the role that they play in the total organization of the city.

Concentric Zone Theory

Perhaps the best-known theory of urban development was the concentric zone theory proposed by Burgess (1925). He stated that a city grows outward in circles from the CBD, the location of the highest land values. The land use most typically found adjacent to the CBD is a zone of transition. This includes wholesale light manufacturing plants and rooming houses for factory workers and transients. Outside of this zone are the working-class homes, including second-generation immigrant settlements. Further out from the CBD is a zone of better residences. Finally, at the borders of the city furthest out from the CBD is the commuters' zone (see Figure 4.1).

Figure 4.1   Three Theories about the Growth of Cities

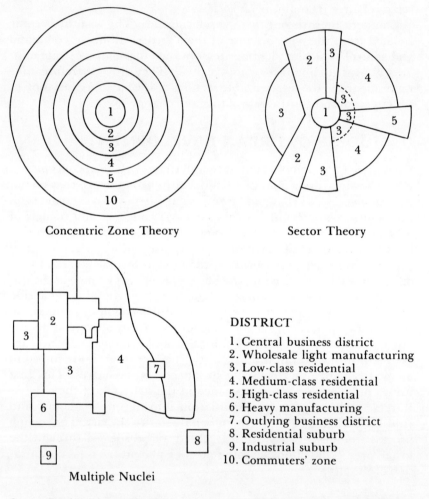

Concentric Zone Theory   Sector Theory

Multiple Nuclei

DISTRICT

1. Central business district
2. Wholesale light manufacturing
3. Low-class residential
4. Medium-class residential
5. High-class residential
6. Heavy manufacturing
7. Outlying business district
8. Residential suburb
9. Industrial suburb
10. Commuters' zone

Source: Reprinted from "The Nature of Cities" by Chauncy D. Harris and Edward L. Ullman, in Volume no. 242 of *The Annals of the American Academy of Political and Social Science* (November, 1945), p. 12.

Immigrant groups tend to settle first in the zone of transition and then, as they prosper, move outwards. Some eventually land in the commuters' zone. The processes of invasion and succession lead to changes over the years in the ethnic character of areas of the city. The transformation of an inner-city area, such as Park Extension in Montreal, from Jewish to Italian to Greek through successive generations of immigrants is an example of how these processes work.

Applying the Burgess concentric zone theory to Canadian cities, Guest (1969) found that urban areas differentiate in their patterns of residential location by socioeconomic groups as cities age and become larger (see Figure 4.1). However, when compared to American cities, Canadian cities are less likely to have a clear pattern of upper-status groups over-represented in the suburbs and lower class groups over-represented in the inner city, as the model predicts. Guest (1969:276) attributes these differences to the fact that Canadian cities tend to be younger and smaller than their American counterparts.

Sector Theory

The concentric zone theory seemed to be an adequate explanation of development of some cities. Upon investigation, however, not all cities appeared to evolve along these lines. An alternative explanation, developed by Hoyt (see Figure 4.1), argues that most residential developments in urban areas of the United States are distributed with respect to commercial and industrial districts of the city (Hoyt, 1939). He states that the general spatial pattern of American cities should be considered in terms of sectors rather than concentric zones. These sectors take on the character of wedges which radiate out from the CBD along transportation routes. These are the locations of commercial and industrial districts. The placement of high-rent residential areas, rather than the CBD, provides the most important organizing factor for urban growth. Their location attracts certain developments (for example, shopping centres) and repels others (for example, heavy industry). An illustration of this is the effect that subway lines have on raising residential values.

Multiple Nuclei Theory

A third perspective of urban development using ecological principles was developed by Harris and Ullman (1945). They propose that land-use patterns in many cities focus on a number of centres. These multiple centres come about through the combination of certain activities that involve specialized facilities, such as transportation. Certain like activities come together because they all profit from concentration (for example, shopping centres). Certain unlike activities are detrimental to each other and thus must be kept separate (industry and residential areas, for example). Finally, some activities that are unable to afford the high rents of more desirable sites in the city, such as specialty stores, drift to the remote centres.

While the specific models were found to have some problems of transference from one city to the next, their basic orientation towards the interplay of ecological processes made them useful to many researchers. The framework that they provided for analyzing city structure and city development provided a much-needed focus for their work. The most enduring model was the concentric zone theory, which typifies to many people the way in which cities evolve from the central business districts out to the suburbs. The land use plans that have emerged in many cities have incorporated this contribution of land form from Burgess. (This was true even though a major criticism of this model was the fact that although Chicago appeared to have evolved in a concentric zone fashion, many other cities did not follow this pattern.)

E. SEGREGATION: INCOME, FAMILY STATUS, AND ETHNICITY

An important area of research that arose from the ecological approach centred around the issues of segregation and change in residential areas. A great deal of research was undertaken to identify the forces of neighbourhood change. Researchers raised the question of the consequences of ecological change for the spatial allocation of groups throughout the city. The focus of this work revolved around the segregation of groups based on ethnic and racial background, economic status, and family status. Of great concern to the early ecologists and to their more contemporary followers is an understanding of the extent and nature of change in city neighbourhoods. Again, however, the ecologists pay little attention to the issue of whether or not this segregation benefited or hindered these groups.

Ethnic Segregation

Canadian studies have looked at these issues of segregation and evolution of neighbourhoods in Canadian cities based on differentiation according to ethnicity, economic status, and family status. Looking first at ethnic segregation, Dreidger (1978) examined ethnic neighbourhoods in Winnipeg. He reports, consistent with the views of the early ecologists, that territory, institutions, and culture are important boundary-maintaining factors in ethnic communities. As change takes place in areas through the process of invasion and succession, new communities are formed and old communities change to suit their new environments.

In Winnipeg, the community of North End which was originally dominated by East European Jews, Ukrainians, and Poles is now experiencing invasion and succession of other ethnic groups. The Jews have moved to the suburbs while the Ukrainians and Poles are losing a clear identity and are giving way to a more heterogeneous, multi-ethnic group of Southern Europeans and Native Indians. In contrast to the North End, the community of North St. Boniface has remained essentially a French neighbourhood for 160 years with little or no outward mobility. This group has resisted both the desire to move elsewhere and the invasion of other groups into their community.

Family Status

According to Hunter and Latif (1973), however, the importance of ethnicity as a factor in creating segregation is not as great in Winnipeg as is family status (including marital status and family size). This finding, they point out, is opposite to what has been found in American cities where major ghettos appear. It points to a trend in the development of Canadian cities which is opposite to what would be expected based on the American experience of ethnic and racial clustering. This finding appears to generalize past Winnipeg, as well. Balakrishnan (1976) finds that in spite of the sustained high immigration and increasing ethnic diversity in Canada, residential segregation is decreasing in Canadian cities.

Economic Segregation

Using an economic perspective, McCann (1975) examined changes in Edmonton's residential structure. He focussed on the importance of housing demand as a basis for explaining neighbourhood transition. The basic demand for housing, based on the Edmonton experience, stems from a continuously expanding population base with groups which either cannot afford or do not desire to live in single-family houses. Combined with this demand is the ability to build apartment blocks quickly and cheaply; the desire by inner-city residents to accrue capital gains in the selling of their houses; the aging of the house and the subsequent decline of neighbourhood upkeep; changing housing and locational preferences of consumers; and public policies to encourage higher-density housing in the inner cities.

Simmons (1974) combines an approach to changes in urban structure based on economic trends with a perspective that considers changes in the life-cycle of the mobile population within the city. In his study of Toronto, he finds that the depopulation of large parts of the older areas of Toronto took place as young households left these areas. This mobility is due primarily to the rise of income levels which permits young people to leave home for an apartment.

They can then move to a suburban area for child-rearing without having to double up with their in-laws. The main source of change in the city, then, is the continuing high rate of net migration of young households away from the core of the city. This creates a series of waves of life-cycle shifts outward from the city centre as people compete for available and suitable housing.

One such group that has to compete for space is the elderly. Golant (1972) reports that, contrary to popular belief, most older movers relocate away from the inner city. This can be attributed to the location of senior citizen residences and to the move to apartments by people leaving their own homes. This mobility, however, is evident most often among the affluent elderly. Those who cannot compete economically for housing are left in areas which are undergoing change and experiencing decay. It is these elderly poor who are creating the most serious problems for social agencies.

The ecologists assume that the allocation of people and resources in the city should take place through natural processes. Problems arise, however, in applying this perspective to situations where there are factors introduced through physical planning which reduce natural competition. Often this planning is done to remove bad living conditions or to satisfy certain global demands for transportation or housing. We will be addressing these issues in detail when we discuss social power and the allocation of resources in Chapter 6. The critics of the ecological perspective pave the way for this discussion. More contemporary ecologists have gone to work to try and address the theory's inadequacies in explaining changes that take place in cities. This work has culminated in an approach referred to as "social area analysis."

F. SOCIAL AREA ANALYSIS

Critics of the ecological theories of urbanization argue that the ecologists tend to view urban development in isolation from the rest of society. For example, the changing conditions of an industrializing society which lead to life-style changes are not accounted for in the ecological explanations of urban settlement. Shevky and Bell (1955) try to overcome these problems. To do this they developed "social area analysis."

Shevky and Bell argue that industrialization leads to three major changes in society: (1) increased rate and intensity of social relations, (2) increased diversity in occupational roles (with consequent effects on family life caused by women entering the labour force), and (3) increased complexity of social organization through the development of social and ethnic segregation. These factors, not just the ecological processes at work in the city, cause changes to take place in urban settlements.

Indices of Social Area Differences

To test this perspective, Shevky and Bell (1955) started with the census characteristics of Los Angeles in 1940. From these they drew three distinct sets of data (indices) which they subsequently used to define urban social areas. The three indices are "social rank," "segregation," and "family status." The social rank index comprises (a) an occupational ratio, based on the proportion of blue-collar workers in an area and (b) an educational ratio, indicating the proportion of adults who have completed less than seven years of schooling. The segregation index consists of the proportion of persons in an area who are foreign-born, Black and non-white.

The family status index comprises (a) the fertility ratio of an area, i.e. the number of children under five years per 1,000 females aged 15 through 44, (b) the "women in the labour force ratio," and (c) the number of single-family houses per 1,000 dwelling units of all types. As a result of these tabulations, each area, usually defined by census tract boundaries, can be assigned three indices. These rank areas with respect to socioeconomic structure, degree of segregation, and level of family status.

Shevky and Bell (1955) argue that, with the growth of cities, the changes in these social area indices reflect changes in the social ecology of the city. Low social rank and low family status are frequently found in an area populated with single men living in inexpensive rooming houses. An area described as high in social rank and low in family status should contain high-cost apartments populated by small families and working women. An area defined as high in family status and low in social rank should be a neighbourhood of families living in single detached houses and having lower-than-average incomes.

Beyond Classification

Social area analysis, despite its initial promise, has been criticized for its inability to provide a better picture of the characteristics of urban social groups than could be produced by using individual census measures. In addition, the approach is heavily oriented towards techniques of mapping social groups. No clearly discernible theory of urban social development has actually emerged from the data analysis.

In an attempt to overcome these limitations and to identify patterns of change of social groups in an urban setting using social area analysis, Murdie (1969) examines the evolution of the City of Toronto from 1951 to 1961. He finds that changes in the city incorporate the characteristics identified by the concentric zone, the sector, and the multiple nuclei theories. Together these three theories can provide an integrated view of that city.

Murdie's findings permit a refinement of the ecological explanation of urbanization (see Figure 4.2). Household attributes and family status are arranged concentrically, as suggested by Burgess. As a result, towards the centre of the city, buildings tend to be older, densities are higher. There is a greater concentration of multiple-unit projects. There is also less private ownership and greater rental accommodation. More women are employed. In addition, there is a greater proportion of older families and fewer children.

Figure 4.2
Idealized Spatial Model of Urban Ecological Structure and Change

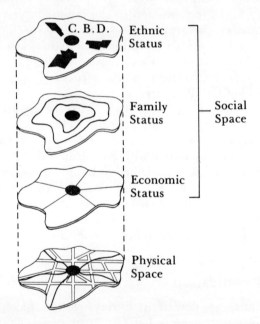

Source: R.A. Murdie, 1969. *Factorial Ecology of Metropolitan Toronto, 1951-66.* Research Paper No. 116, Department of Geography Research Series, University of Chicago. Figure 1.

Economic status and social rank have a sectorial distribution, as argued by Hoyt (1939). The lower the incomes, the closer the homes are to places of work. Poorer neighbourhoods tend to be located in poor-quality sections adjoining industrial and transportation zones. High-income areas follow the placement of amenities suitable for higher quality housing, such as golf courses and open spaces. Finally, segregation, on an ethnic basis, cuts across both the concentric zones and the transportation routes. The ethnic clustering is based on concentration of schools, ethnic-based facilities, and ethnic institutions. This leads to the development of multiple nuclei. The Italian and Jewish enclaves in Toronto are clear examples of these areas.

Schwirian and Matre (1974) tested the principles of social area analysis on the ecological structure of 11 Canadian cities by testing propositions based on findings from U.S. cities (see Tables 4.1 and 4.2). They found that the basic technique worked when applied to the Canadian context. In Table 4.1, social rank is represented by a combination of occupational and educational levels by census tracts in each city. Ethnicity is measured by the concentration of English language versus others. Familism (or family status) is multidimensional, so two analyses are presented. The combined index of familism based on measures of infertility (i.e., a measure of fertility), women in the labour force and people living in multiple-family dwellings is presented in Table 4.1. The analysis of each of these familism measures separately is presented in Table 4.2. The analysis on spatial distribution studies the level of concentration of these characteristics by sector and distance. Each city is divided into 12 sectors of 30 degrees width. Distance is measured by the location of the census tract from the city centre. In the two tables, high percentages indicate that an index has a particular spatial characteristic.

Table 4.1.

Percent of the Total Sum of Squares of Social Area Analysis Variables Explained by Sectors and by Distance for 11 Canadian Cities

City	Social Rank		Familism		Ethnicity	
	Sector	Distance	Sector	Distance	Sector	Distance
Calgary	44.7	17.1	35.7*	41.8*	17.5	22.7
Edmonton	31.7*	50.8*	2.7	93.6*	13.0	62.0*
Hamilton	64.8*	0.8	11.7*	82.1*	71.6*	15.0
London	62.0*	5.0	5.9	75.0*	36.3	23.2
Montréal	52.8*	19.5	11.5*	79.6*	50.0	9.9
Ottawa	22.6	29.3	21.0*	64.6*	81.5*	8.4
Québec	67.4*	0.5	19.5	50.0*	93.2*	0.6
Toronto	62.8*	11.2	11.7	41.6	16.2	72.9*
Vancouver	35.1	15.6	15.6	57.6*	17.2	39.4
Windsor	18.0	34.8	31.7*	56.0*	28.4	18.2
Winnipeg	68.6*	5.6	6.5	78.5*	17.6	49.1*

* The percentage of the sum of squares is statistically significant beyond the .05 level. The test of significance is the two-way analysis of variance.
Source: Schwirian and Marc Matre in *Comparative Urban Structure: Studies in the Ecology of Cities*, edited by Kent P. Schwirian. Copyright © 1973 by D.C. Heath and Company, Reprinted by permission of the publisher.

Table 4.2.

Percent of the Total Sum of Squares of the Components of the Familism Index Explained by Sectors and by Distance for 11 Canadian Cities

City	Infertility		Women in Labor Force		Multiple Dwelling Units	
	Sector	Distance	Sector	Distance	Sector	Distance
Calgary	24.0*	61.0*	39.7	26.2	37.8	25.9
Edmonton	3.4	85.3*	4.5	86.4*	1.6	80.9*
Hamilton	27.0	38.7	25.1*	61.7*	8.9	83.0*
London	46.9*	24.5	2.0	71.2*	3.1	82.2*
Montréal	16.0	60.7*	13.8*	78.5*	21.7	49.5*
Ottawa	35.1	24.9	9.6	74.2*	19.8	50.3*
Québec	26.2*	60.9*	28.7	14.2	4.4	64.8*
Toronto	69.2*	12.7	39.9*	14.8	6.1	71.8*
Vancouver	61.0*	4.7	22.6	24.1	5.2	76.5*
Windsor	3.6	6.3	32.6	30.4	31.5*	61.1*
Winnipeg	24.6	54.3*	6.5	76.3*	7.9	84.6*

* The percentage of the sum of squares is statistically significant at the .05 level. The test of significance is the two-way analysis of variance.

Source: "The Ecological Structure of Canadian Cities" by Kent P. Schwirian and Marc Matre in *Comparative Urban Structure: Studies in the Ecology of Cities*, edited by Kent P. Schwirian. Copyright © 1973 by D.C. Heath and Company. Reprinted by permission of the publisher.

When looking at the results we find, first, that the Canadian city structure is described by vectors which correspond to the concepts of social rank, familism, and ethnicity. Second, the spatial patterning of these three dimensions varies. Social rank is distributed by sector while familism is distributed by distance from the city centre in concentric zones. The distribution of ethnicity, meanwhile, varies considerably from one city to the next. Of interest in these findings, as well, is the emergence of regional variations in the degree of correlation of the ethnicity and social rank vectors. These are more closely related in the Eastern cities of Canada than is the case in the West.

This descriptive analysis of change in the character of the city has little focus on the actual behaviour that takes place in the areas that are affected by ecological processes. Some attempts to deal with this issue of behaviour have developed around the concern about crime in the city. The "ecology of crime" develops as an important subarea of research in the ecological literature, as a result. We can now turn to a discussion of this research to highlight the way in which ecologists treat the consequences of behavioural change in cities and maladaptation of residents to their environments.

G. THE ECOLOGY OF CRIME

Mapping Urban Pathology

The pathologies in cities that developed with constant changes in social and physical structure were seen by ecologists as products of the same subsocial forces that created natural areas in cities. As Michelson (1975) explains, according to the Burgess concentric zone theory, the concentration of vice and gambling just outside the Central Business District results from the high land values associated with the growth of the CBD. The constant growth of this district encourages speculators to purchase property on its periphery in anticipation of eventual incorporation into the core area. So as to minimize expenses and maximize short-term profits, the interim landlords hold older property without improving it. These properties are turned into rooming houses which in turn attract newcomers to the city who cannot afford any other accommodation. The atmosphere created in these transient areas becomes one of minimal commitment. There is little personal contact and low levels of external social control. Crime and personal breakdown result. The underlying factors creating this situation are the economic determinants of urban change and development (Michelson, 1975:9).

This argument led to the mapping of crime areas in the city. This was done to provide pictures of the factors which lead to social pathology and crime. Faris and Dunham (1939) did this type of work in mapping the areas of schizophrenia in the Chicago area. This pattern of mental disorder coincided with the concentric zone model. Using this technique, they found that schizophrenia consistently decreased outwardly from the core area of the city.

The ecological perspective on crime has had effects on popular thinking about crime patterns in cities. It has been discussed in planning, police deployment, and social service delivery. It has also made its way into public discussions of crime. The temptation of drawing a relationship between geographical incidence of crime and individual characteristics of people living in areas can lead to some tenuous conclusions. In an article published in 1974, the *Toronto Star* printed a discussion of the recently released crime statistics for the city. As these statistics were provided to the paper according to geographical areas, the reporter wrote the article to discuss these rates in the context of the characteristics of particular areas.

In describing the relatively high crime rates for the police district containing the Annex area in Toronto, the paper described this area as owing its reputation to the mobile nature of its residents.

It's home to students in cooperative housing, the chic
young professional set who want the renovated town-
houses, many members of the city's drug subculture and
those people "just passing through" living in the area's
many rooming houses.

And it's the transients who make life most difficult for
police and law-abiding citizens, police say" (*Toronto
Star*, Mar 22, 1974:3).

The problem with this type of analysis is that it conveys the
impression that in this high crime rate area, all transients (including
students) are committing all of the crime. The labelling of the area
as criminal implies that the majority of people living there are criminal. There is no way of isolating any particular group which may,
in fact, be committing all of the crimes. It may be the case that this
high crime rate occurs in this area because the people here are being
victimized by burglars or muggers who are coming into the area
from other parts of the city. The people here may be easier targets
for crime than are people elsewhere. Attaching the characteristics
of people in an area to certain behaviour, such as crime, is a hazard-
ous practice and has been labelled the "ecological fallacy" (Robinson, 1950).

Robinson illustrated the methodological problems of failing to
distinguish between individual and social levels of analysis. In one of
his studies, he found that for individual cases there was a small
"positive" correlation between nativity and illiteracy. That is, persons who were foreign born tended to be illiterate slightly more
often than the native-born samples he studied. Meanwhile, when
the relationship between nativity and illiteracy was examined by
regions in the United States, a moderately strong "negative" relationship appeared. In other words, those regions of the country with
high proportions of foreign-born residents tended to have low rates
of illiteracy. What this illustates is that the same variables can relate
differently according to the units of analysis involved. What is true
for the individual is not necessarily true for the group and vice versa.

Crime and Routine Activities

Recent discussions of the ecology of crime have moved away from an
explanation of crime according to the characteristics of areas defined by their occupants. This later work has emphasized instead
the routine character of activities in the urban area which offer targets for crime. As Felson and Cohen (1980) state, the interdepend-
ence between offenders and victims can be viewed as a symbiotic
predatory relationship. Illegal activities must feed on other activities. Therefore, the spatial and temporal structure of routine

legitimate activities should play an important role in determining the location, type, and quantity of illegal acts in a given community or society. Routine daily activities affect the likelihood that property and personal targets will be both visible and accessible to illegitimate activities. These activities will also determine whether personal targets have high visibility and accessibility at particular times.

The central empirical argument of this perspective is that the changing structure of North American society may have contributed to declines in the "tempo" of primary group activity (including contact with neighbours and friends) within households. This has occurred with people leaving their homes in order to pursue their daily tasks. This, in turn, appears to have led to a convergence of criminal behaviour in communities. Basically, it is not criminal inclination alone which is the root of increases in crime. Rather, several other factors contribute to this. These include the tools, skills, and weapons available to the offenders; the suitability of targets; the protection of targets by people; the spatio-temporal distribution of people having criminal inclinations; and the timing of their activities with those of targets and guardians (Felson and Cohen, 1980:397).

The introduction of ecological variables in explaining the incidence of crime from an "activity" perspective raises some interesting research questions and some practical concerns about crime prevention. The setting which is available to the offender who is "casing the joint" becomes an important consideration in determining the likelihood of victimization. Plotting trends in these characteristics across the urban environment should provide important insights into the factors that are most important in predicting victimization. The practical decisions concerning surveillance or "hardening targets" will obviously benefit from this analysis. The deployment of police to interrupt this attempt to take advantage of changing tempo in peoples' activities is also a practical consideration coming out of this research. The ecology of crime will obviously be an important area of research in future years.

H. CRITICISMS OF THE ECOLOGICAL PERSPECTIVE

Despite these attempts to improve the ecological research of the city using social variables, as in the study of crime, many weaknesses of the approach remain. Michelson (1975) outlines some basic problems with the ecological perspective. He points out that the ecologists pay no attention to the physical environment of the city. They treat it as a medium rather than a variable with its own effects on social behaviour. Any attempt to rectify this omission is precluded by the ecologists' insistence on looking at only the arrangement of social aggregates in space. They assume that the questions of the physical environment's effects go beyond the boundaries of the discipline of human ecology.

Second, human ecology relies on information about social aggregates mainly derived from census counts. This leads to the study of aggregates of people rather than of individuals themselves. Individuals define their own communities. These definitions are ignored by the ecologists, in whose eyes communities are real only as they are defined by census groupings used in the analysis of data. This type of analysis leads to the "ecological fallacy" discussed above. For example, can we assume that all people living in high-crime areas are criminals?

Finally, the assumption in ecology that cities evolve according to some natural order ignores the effects that urban design and planning have had in bringing about changes in urban forms and urban settlements. These changes may be seen as resulting from the choices that people make in selecting the environments where they want to live. Alternatively, changes may be due to restrictive city policies placed on the distribution of services in certain areas.

The ecologists generally study how urban structure evolves as a result of migration into the city and the economics of land use. The questions that they raise, but fail to answer, are: (1) "What is the effect of city life on peoples' relationships with friends or relatives, their recreational pastimes, and their work?"; (2) "How do people adapt to social and physical conditions in cities?"; (3) "How do natural processes affect the distribution of people in terms of their search for high-quality environments?"; and (4) "How are the concerns about the fair access to decent housing, safety, and community support ensured in environments where competition means the survival of the fittest?" The answers to these questions serve as the major focus of the researchers who emphasize opportunity and choice in the evolution of urban environments.

I. SUMMARY AND CONCLUSIONS

From the initial work that was done in Chicago, the urban ecologists developed a number of principles for describing how cities develop and change. Basic to these changes is competition. Just as organisms compete in the natural environment, so people compete in the urban environment for resources and space. The geographic distribution of people is shaped into "natural areas" or neighbourhoods where people with similar backgrounds based on ethnicity, family status, or income gather.

The forces of competition underlie seven ecological processes bringing about change in cities. These include centralization, decentralization, concentration, deconcentration, segregation, invasion, and succession. These processes were incorporated into models of urban development devised by ecologists to explain the changing structure of cities. These models include a concentric- zone theory, a sector theory, and a multiple-nuclei theory. Each of these models provided descriptions of urban structure but not any one was adequate in describing all cities. The importance of these demographic characteristics in bringing about segregation in cities was also investigated by the ecologists.

The descriptive models of urban development were limited in their ability to explain how individuals adapted to city life. It was difficult to explain the reasons for social pathology or changes in urban life styles using these models. Social area analysis was devised as a way of identifying urban neighbourhoods according to the characteristics of their residents and then making some statement about the variations in life style in these areas. The changes in the division of labour in society were most important in providing the theoretical rationale behind social area analysis. Murdie's (1969) research of Toronto proposed that the application of the three models based on differences in income, family status, and ethnicity provided the most meaningful picture of urban change. Despite its initial promise, however, difficulties arose with social area analysis doing little more than simply mapping areas in cities according to the demographic characteristics of residents. Little could be said about their behaviour using this approach.

This problem of analyzing behaviour proved to be a major criticism of the ecological approach. Also, the ecologists tended to ignore the physical environment in their research, thereby making it difficult to understand the importance of planning in undermining the ecological processes which were supposedly operating solely on the basis of natural competition.

The ecological perspective has been used in mapping crime patterns. Also, it is useful in understanding the changes in cities that take place on the basis of activities that occur routinely throughout the urban environment. Ecology has been influential in its emphasis on the interaction between urban populations and their spatial surroundings. Despite its limitations, it provides an important theoretical base for dealing with the distribution of different populations throughout the city.

5 Social Choice and the Voluntaristic Perspective

A. THREE THEORIES OF SOCIAL CHOICE

Urbanism as a Way of Life

The ecologists see cities as organisms in which urban processes compete to create different social and physical structures. The point of view that evolved from this work concentrated analysis at the institutional level rather than on individual change. Wirth (1938:9) argues that: "the central problem of the sociologist of the city is to discover the forms of social action and organization that typically emerge in relatively permanent, compact settlements of large numbers of heterogeneous individuals." He adds that: "The larger, the more densely populated, and the more heterogeneous a community, the more accentuated the characteristics associated with urbanism," such as loneliness and social breakdown, will be.

This urbanism results from bringing together individuals who have no sentimental or emotional ties to one another. There is a spirit of competition, aggrandizement, and exploitation. Wirth's view of urbanism is in keeping with the perspective of the human ecologists. To counteract irresponsibility and potential disorder, the society reverts to formal controls. According to Wirth (1938:16), this formal order is exemplified by the clock and traffic lights. Frequent close physical contact, coupled with great social distance, accentuates the reserve of these unattached individuals towards one another. Unless there is some compensation offered through these informal contacts, the individual is faced with loneliness. Personal disorganization, mental breakdown, suicide, delinquency, crime, corruption, and disorder are more prevalent in cities than in small towns or rural areas. Wirth infers that such problems derive in part from the depersonalizing effects of city size, density, and heterogeneity.

80

Within the urban structure, Wirth argues, there is a deadening monotony for the individual trapped by the need to work at unpleasant jobs to meet the high costs of city living. To escape this the individual turns to formal organizations where people of similar backgrounds and interests are found. The predictability of rural associations imbedded in tradition disappears. These are replaced with a complicated network of social institutions and organizations which form to serve individual needs. Because of their loosely knit framework, however, institutions lose formal control of behaviour. This results in problems of social disorganization and breakdown.

The simplicity of Wirth's argument and its appeal to those who truly believe that the city is a place of moral and social breakdown made it central to the thinking of urbanologists for many years. This view was not inconsistent with that offered by the antiurbanists whom we discussed in an earlier chapter. Over the years, however, Wirth's theory of urbanism became the centre of controversy. Many researchers saw Wirth's perspective as providing an empirically testable set of propositions about the factors which bring about urbanism as a way of life. Others, however, pointed out that his belief in the unidimensional effects of urban life on the traditional values of small town and rural life led him to ignore the complexity of cities. His argument was based specifically on the ecological change brought about in societies by the dominance of the city over the rural areas, coupled with the changing characteristics of types and location of work. Wirth believed that the movement of people to cities brought about ecological changes which resulted in changes in the way in which society functioned. He saw the demise of traditional values as simply a function of the change in the ecological distribution of people of different backgrounds in a crowded metropolis.

Individual Choice

In response to this point of view, three theoretical frameworks emerged which argued against the societal focus of the ecology school. They emphasized, instead, the importance of individual choice in determining the nature of urban social structure. The three perspectives incorporate the work by Herbert Gans, William Michelson and Claude Fischer. These three perspectives can be seen as each addressing the issues raised in Wirth's theory of urbanism by focussing on how individual choice, rather than ecological sorting, brings about distinct urban life styles.

Life styles are based on "role emphasis" (Michelson, 1975:62). People can assume the role of father or businessman, mother or professional. The emphasis that people put on the role that they are playing dictates the nature of the activities in which they involve themselves. It also influences choices of environments. Two elements are included in life style. One is a set of behaviours which must be performed to satisfy a role. This often includes social interaction with other people. The other is the sphere of life which is emphasized at the time the role is being played. These spheres of life include political behaviour, economic behaviour, raising children, and recreation.

Gans on Social Homogeneity

Gans (1970:78) argues that: "Ecological explanations of social life are most applicable if the subjects under study lack the ability to *make choices*." If people have choices, however, they will respond to them based on an attempt to meet their own explicit demands. These demands, he argues, can be best understood in terms of the characteristics of the people involved. The most important of these include social class and stage in the family life cycle. Based on the way in which people group according to these characteristics, they will adopt different styles of living in the city. These groups have informal support systems and do not suffer from the negative aspects of urban life attributed to them by Wirth. Gans argues strongly against Wirth's concept that heterogeneity brings about alienation. According to Gans, Wirth ignores the opportunities that people make for themselves based on commonalities of social class and life cycle.

Gans (1970:72) states that while it is true that a significant proportion of the inner-city population is made up of unattached individuals (a problem which Wirth argued led to a breakdown in informal social control), Wirth ignores the fact that these people live in areas where they are surrounded by people who are like them. The creation of inner-city neighbourhoods populated by young professionals; the evolution of suburban areas which attract people with children; the restoration of ethnic enclaves drawing people of similar backgrounds to live, shop, and play in these areas all provided examples for Gans to illustrate the basic homogeneity of groups within urban areas.

Gans argues that the urban way of life described by Wirth is most appropriately applied to the transient areas of the inner city. These areas are heterogeneous in population partly because they are inhabited by transients who do not require homogeneous neighbourhoods. Alternatively, they may contain deprived people who have no choice or may themselves be mobile. Under these conditions of transience and heterogeneity people interact only in terms of segmental roles required for acquiring local services. As a result, social relationships become characterized by anonymity, impersonality, and superficiality. But these characteristics of social breakdown are not products of the structural change from rural to urban society, as argued by Wirth. Rather they are a result of residential instability. In other, more stable parts of the city, the homogeneous neighbourhoods create the kind of social cohesion that brings about social support and social interaction, with informal methods of social control.

Fischer on City Size

Fischer (1975b), meanwhile, accepts Gans' view that the values of the subgroup to which people belong determine their behaviour. However, he sees a role that the opportunities offered by large community size and structural differentiation play in encouraging the development of these subcultures. The ecological changes talked about by Wirth are not constraints on choice, forcing people into alienating and monotonous environments. Rather, the diversity afforded by large cities creates opportunities to pursue life styles not available in rural areas and small towns. The simple fact that economies of scale allow particular subgroups to follow their interests argues for the possibility that subcultures can grow and flourish in cities. This does not mean social breakdown. Rather, a new social order arises to accommodate these new interests.

This point of view is underlined by the argument by Milgram (1977) that people in cities tend to respond to the overload to their senses by becoming non-responsive to many things around them, including the large number of strangers whom they meet constantly. However there is, underlying this, a form of adaptation that takes place where new norms of behaviour are developed and implemented. The impersonality of city life breeds its own tolerance for the private lives of individuals. Individuality and eccentricity (seen by Wirth as negated by the urban environment) can in fact flourish in cities more than in small towns. The acceptance of deviant lifestyles is more readily obtained. In fact, this deviance is sometimes promoted by the protection that comes with the presence of large numbers of people living in an area that share this life style (Milgram, 1977:102).

Michelson on Density and Environment

Michelson (1975:40) goes further and argues that not only institutional structures but also the physical structure of individual environments are important in creating opportunities for the adoption by various groups of different life styles. The density issues that Wirth stresses are important, in Michelson's view, but only as they facilitate social choice.

The city environment consists of a variety of physical characteristics. All of these can affect the ways in which people work and play. It is the desire for certain types of activities that leads people to seek out environments conducive to these behaviours. The role of planners and architects in designing these environments is important in establishing a congruence of individual needs and expectations with physical structures.

All three of these "choice" perspectives emphasize the role of the individual and the demands that life styles place on the social and physical fabric of the city. In arguing against Wirth and the ecologists, the choice theorists find themselves concentrating on the contention that urban environments are socially alienating. The negative aspects of urban life were seen by Wirth to arise from the loss of close social contact and social support from friends, neighbours, and relatives in the move from rural communities to urban ones. This is a point that we reviewed extensively in discussing the research on the rural-urban continuum. We can examine how Fischer, Gans, and Michelson have addressed this concern as it is basic to the issue of social choice and the focus on the individual.

B. SUBCULTURES AND SOCIAL INTERACTION

Subcultural Theory

Fischer (1976:36) underlines the importance of the role that subcultures within the city play in affecting the adaptation of people. He states that urbanism, which equates to increased community complexity, affects social life by helping to create and strengthen social groups. The "subcultural theory" holds that with increasing city size, there is the increasing likelihood of subcultures being allowed to thrive. These subcultures consist of people who share relatively distinctive traits (like ethnicity or occupation). They especially interact with one another. They also share a distinct set of beliefs and behaviours. The subcultural theory states, further, that groups are affected directly by the changing character of the urban environment. Changes in the size of the community are important but not because increased size destroys social worlds. Rather, it creates opportunities for them to thrive.

There are two ways in which urbanism has its effects on subcultural groups. First, large communities attract migrants from wider areas than do small towns. These migrants bring with them wide varieties of cultural backgrounds and traditions. Second, large size produces structural differentiation. Subcultures are usually attached to each of the specialized institutions (Fischer, 1976:37). Examples of these are the police, students, and people with shared political beliefs. It is no longer the case, as was emphasized by Poplin, that people share all parts of their lives, as they do in rural homogeneous areas. As Fischer says, urbanism generates a variety of social worlds.

An area of emphasis in Fischer's work is the influence of the structural characteristics of cities on the social networks and social support systems that people have available to them. Related to the issue of adaptation to the city is the extent to which people find themselves cut off from others similar to them. Louis Wirth and others argue that the consequences of growth in settlements, specifically their increased density and their increased heterogeneity, are increased social disorganization and alienation. Fischer (1976:38) argues, using his subcultural theory, that this is not the case. Increased city size simply allows for a greater diversity of cultural groups. There is, as a result, a greater amount of choice in social contact.

In large cities, says Fischer, the options that people have lead them to choose social support that is not spatially bounded. While the quality of the contact that people have may differ according to the ecological character of the city, this is not dependent on geographical constraints. Unlike rural communities, those in large cities are freer to avoid social contacts with others. In fact, avoidance is a function of both distrust and independence from those in physical proximity. Trust is placed instead on those who are more alike socially, but who are not necessarily geographically close.

Liberated Communities

Wellman and Leighton (1979) refer to these types of social contact as emanating from the "liberated community." The structural and technological changes in urban society have liberated communities from the confines of neighbourhoods. They have dispersed network ties from all-embracing communities to ones that are more narrowly based. The changes that allow the networks of this type to thrive include (1) cheap, effective transportation and communication facilities; (2) the separation of workplace and kinship ties into nonlocal networks; and (3) high rates of social and residential mobility (Wellman and Leighton, 1979:377). People can live in different parts of town, then, but maintain strong ties with people who are like them across town.

In Fischer's (1981) research, consistent with the hypothesis about freedom from proximity, he found that the likelihood of having family within walking distance declined with an increase in city size. Friends and family are equally present in the city as in the rural areas. However, they are more widely distributed over space in the city (Fischer, 1981:312). In sum, social isolation is only weakly associated with urbanism. The more urban the place, the less local are one's interpersonal contacts.

In their study of Leaside in Toronto, Wellman and Leighton (1979) report that liberated communities are evident among the people living there. Ties with people outside the neighbourhood are the most intense of all the contacts that people have. They do not always have the functional specificity that local ties have (e.g. getting a neighbour to help with the plumbing) but are more broadly based in providing social, moral, and financial support to the individual.

Suburban Communities

Fischer and Jackson (1976) pursue this same theme in an investigation of suburbs. They argue that, consistent with the major thrust of Fischer's subcultural theory, factors in the environment, such as density or location, would lead to changes in the types of adaptation that people make to these environments. They work with three basic assumptions in this analysis. First, the direct social effects of population concentration result from achieving a critical mass within distinctive subcultures. Second, personality, attitudes, and behaviour are to a great extent determined by the content and structure of individuals' personal social networks. Third, people choose network associates and continue interaction with them as a positive function of commonalities and as a negative function of the cost of the interaction (Fischer and Jackson, 1976:281).

In the case of the suburbs, this cost is calculated on the basis of the distances covered and time expended in travelling to meet with associates and friends. As Fischer and Jackson point out, distance means little except insofar as it is translated into access. They are interested in access from an individual's home to gathering places of people who are his or her real and potential associates. So, within an ideal-type metropolis which is circular in shape and in which the density declines from the centre, the further one is from the centre, the greater the average distance to other persons.

With these principles in mind, Fischer and Jackson (1976:282) make the prediction that the personal networks of suburban residents will tend to be more localized than those of city dwellers. That is, suburbanites' close associates and social activities will be located closer to their homes than is the case for inner-city dwellers. In analyzing a cross-national study in the United States, they found that there were small differences between inner-city and suburban dwellers in terms of the nature and extent of their social interaction with associates. Suburban effects, they claim, were quite small (Fischer and Jackson, 1976:304). If one were to try to increase contacts with neighbours, for example, increasing suburbanization would probably not be effective. What would be more effective would be to examine the self-selection process that people go through in choosing suburbs in the first place.

Research done on the evolution of Canadian suburbs has found a similar lack of support for the argument that suburbanization, rather than the types of people who live in suburbs, contributes to changes in the community attachment which develops in these areas. Clark (1966), in his study of the evolution of the suburbs of Toronto, concluded that while the suburbs were still new, they attracted a wide range of people. This attraction was based on many different reasons, such as cost of housing and a desire for new environments for raising children. The specific character of these suburbs, a character which was often intentionally designed by the planners to attract a certain type of person, tended to get lost as these areas developed. As the land around the suburban developments became built up with the same services provided to all areas, there ceased to be anything that distinguished these areas from the older established urban residential ones. The distinguishing feature became, not the location, but rather the people who came to live there. It was this factor, Clark (1966:90) maintains, that created unique areas.

An important addendum to Clark's findings is the fact that suburbs did differ from inner-city neighbourhoods in terms of self-selection based on income. This came as a result of the exclusionary effects of high-priced land and housing. Comparative work done in the United States, however, has concluded that consistent with what has been found with upper-income suburbs, lower-income suburbs have similar characteristics to inner-city areas (Whyte, 1956). The most important factor in bringing about social contact and social support in these studies is social homogeneity.

In Vancouver, Hardwick (1974) reports similar findings concerning the evolution and development of suburban neighbourhoods. Three primary groups have been identified in the Vancouver suburbs which give these areas distinctive characteristics. The dominant group occupying the west end of the city was defined as the "eastern Canadians." This group comprised that segment of the population which came from mercantile and managerial backgrounds and was typified by the settlements in the Point Grey area. In contrast, a second group which largely comprised organized labour drawn from British working-class backgrounds, spread into the Mount Pleasant and South Vancouver districts. The minority ethnic populations, particularly the Asians, concentrated in the inner east side (Hardwick, 1974:113-117).

These areas were seen as being not only distinctive in terms of their residential characteristics, but also unique in terms of the extent to which people living there shared social beliefs and identified these areas as places of primary socialization. As Hardwick (1974:116) explains, areas similar in an outward way obscure more interesting variation. For example, areas with similar incomes, house values, rents, and the same physical appearance attract occupational groups with expectations of high upward social mobility.

At the same time other areas attract tradesmen. He underlines the point made above that social homogeneity in terms of social characteristics and life styles determines the characteristics of suburban areas. Not all suburbs are the same.

C. SOCIAL HOMOGENEITY AND SOCIAL INTERACTION

Life Style and Social Pathology in the Inner City

As outlined above, Gans (1970) argues that Wirth's (1938) generalization that the urban community is socially alienating when compared to rural life does not recognize the fact that many different life-style groups are found in urban areas.

In writing about social pathology, Gans reacts to the argument put forth by Wirth that increased size and density of cities leads to a breakdown of social control over individual behaviour. He argues that this breakdown came as a result of the individual's economic or emotional state. It was not a result of increasing density in cities. Here social pathology is seen as a result of socio-emotional characteristics of the urbanites, rather than coming as a result of increased pressure brought to bear on people by the press of large numbers of people.

Gans (1970:72) justifies this position by outlining the fact that within the inner city, where the density levels are at their highest, there are five different groups. Gans points out that these five groups of urbanites all live in dense and heterogeneous surroundings. Yet they have highly diverse ways of life and make very different adjustments to the environment. It is difficult to see how density and heterogeneity could exert a common influence. The five groups include people living a cosmopolitan life style; unmarried or childless couples; "ethnic villagers"; the deprived; and the trapped or downwardly mobile. Gans (1970:73) argues that when people with social ties based on criteria other than mere common occupancy (e.g. living in the same high-rise development) live together, they can form communities based on their common characteristics, such as ethnicity. This happens regardless of the physical closeness of their neighbours.

The first three groups are in the inner city by choice. Gans defines cosmopolites as including students, artists, writers and professionals who choose to live in the inner city for its good accessibility to cultural facilities. He states that the unmarried or childless use the city as a place of temporary residence and tend to live in apartments. The "ethnic villagers" cluster together into areas where they isolate themselves from the rest of the city. Their way of life differs sharply from Wirth's urbanism in that it does emphasize kinship, the primary group, and the lack of anonymity (Gans, 1970).

As pointed out earlier, Breton (1968) found, contrary to the expectations that immigrants find the host society alienating, that urban ethnic groups in Montreal provide their own institutions, schools, churches, and clubs. An "institutional completeness" occurs in order to insulate members from the culture shock of adapting to a new society. Urbanism for these groups, then, is heavily influenced by the cultural norms and values of the ethnic group. Individual migrants need not feel alienated nor fend for themselves without the assistance of ethnic organizations to make their adaptation easier.

Social Networks

Wellman, et al. (1970), using social networks as a way of defining community structure (that is, looking at differences between relationships with friends and relatives versus contacts with acquaintances, shopkeepers, and the like) found that there is a strong set of networks in place to provide everyday support. Also, emergency networks (needed during illness, for example) are available to individuals living in cities. This support derives from primary relationships with friends, neighbours, and relatives. Analysis done on the data collected in Leaside in Toronto supports Gans' view that patterns of interaction are defined by differences in the social characteristics of the individuals and of the neighbourhoods in which they live.

In terms of individual comparisons, Shulman (1975:318) reports that there are variations by age and life-cycle in the composition, stability, patterns of contact, and exchange in the social networks that people maintain, with kin, friends, and neighbours. Single young adults are less likely to count kin as among their closest relationships. They compensate instead through contact with friends who relate to them in terms of their work and companionship. People who reach a stage in life in which the spouse and children are central features emphasize contact with kin over friends and neighbours.

However, these individual effects can be altered by neighbourhood characteristics. Again from the same study, Wayne (1972:90) reports that neighbouring increases for the white-collar workers, the predominant group in this area. In addition, taking all classes together, kinship participation goes up as class level declines. This finding is also reported in working-class neighbourhoods in Hamilton (Pineo, 1966).

These findings, however, are conditional on the social characteristics of the neighbourhoods. This is consistent with Gans' perspective. Wayne (1972:84) found that in terms of seeing kin, the neigh-

bourhood context has a marked effect. Blue-collar kinship participation is relatively unaffected by whether they live in blue- collar or
white-collar areas. However, the white-collar respondents' participation with kin is affected by the social context of the neighbourhood. White-collar kinship participation declines as neighbourhood
class goes up (Wayne, 1972:90).

Relatively speaking, when they live in areas where there are people like them young couples without children see kin more. However, people at other stages of the life cycle see kin less. Young
couples who live in areas of high concentrations of family households see friends less than do those in low family-oriented neighbourhoods. However, those in the other stages of the life cycle see
friends more.

The interaction between the type of neighbourhood and the type
of person is also reflected in neighbouring. Those at the childrear-
ing stage generally do more neighbouring than do single young
adults and childless couples. These findings prove true in all of the
different kinds of neighbourhoods. Even for those families where
the children have left home, when they live in areas where there are
a high proportion of families with children, they see a great deal of
their neighbours. Meanwhile, those who live in areas without
families see little of their neighbours.

These findings underscore the role that social homogeneity plays
in affecting the bonding that people are able to achieve with others.
Gans (1961:178) argues that this interaction comes as a result of opportunities afforded by homogeneity. They are not due to any other
factors such as location or house and neighbourhood design. People
interact, then, because they find others who are like them, not
because the physical environment or the size of community determines this interaction.

Social Mix in Suburbs

Gans (1970:76) applied his analysis of cultural groups further to a
study of suburban areas outside of the city. His purpose was to compare suburbanites with inner-city residents, much as earlier researchers had examined rural-urban differences. At the time of his
studies, suburbs were characterized by writers such as Riesman
(1958) as areas of "suburban sadness" due to loneliness. Gans
(1970:76) found contrary evidence to these effects in his research.
Where people are homogeneous in terms of income, occupation, or
education, there is a greater likelihood that sociability between
neighbours will result. This is the first step in creating informal
social networks. The suburbs that Gans studied exhibited these
traits of homogeneity. The social relationships that many thought
were missing in suburbs were, in fact, very strong and viable.

Moreover, Gans (1970:81) concludes, social homogeneity within life-style groups is the most important factor in the creation of communities and the maintenance of social relationships. The differences between single-family versus high-rise dwellings or urban versus suburban locations *per se* do not affect social relations just as rural versus urban location does not affect social relations. A sense of community arises where people share similar characteristics, whether they live in rural areas, in cities or in suburbs.

Saved Communities

Wellman and Leighton (1979) refer to neighbourhood networks as part of the "saved community." The local support that people derive from neighbours and friends in close proximity to them is important for help in day-to-day activities and in emergencies. These contacts comprise only a minority, albeit an important part, of a person's network ties. The aspatial, "liberated community" takes up the majority of people's time and resources to maintain. Neighbourhood relationships persist only as specialized components of the overall primary networks that individuals have with other people (Wellman and Leighton, 1979:385).

D. ENVIRONMENT AND SOCIAL INTERACTION

Individual and Institutional Measurement

Michelson (1975:44) argues that studying the city from the point of view of aggregate change obscures the understanding of how cities change individual behaviour. In addition, it does not allow us to understand how various individual groups contribute to institutional change. It is easier to combine minute observations into a large group than to break down observations into more detailed factors if they have not been measured in this way in the first place. For example, if we ask people their incomes according to actual dollar amounts, we can group this information in hundreds or thousands of dollars. If we ask for income in thousands of dollars, we will never know the exact income of respondents.

The problem with institutional measurement, as practised by the ecologists, goes beyond reification. It extends as well into the area of measuring individual adaptation according to the values and goals of the group to which the individuals belong. Michelson explains that to gather a systematic set of concepts that build a socially relevant picture of the environment, both at the individual and institutional level, we must begin with concepts that have meaning for the individuals that live in the city.

Congruence

As Michelson (1975:26) conceives of this process, the interplay between individual values and the environment seeks to achieve some level of congruence. This congruence is sought by the individual through the process of independent decisions about the suitability of environments and the opportunities that they provide to achieve certain desired goals.

Michelson starts with the premise that people are separated in space from other people. This separation is different, however, from that proposed by the human ecologists. The ecologists look at the issues of the mixtures of land use and the distinctions of focal points in metropolitan areas. The individual level of analysis looks at the distances that people have to travel between these sites, rather than the locations of the sites *per se*. It also looks at the adaptation that people are able to make to high-density living, suburban location, and other variations in the environment. These are viewed in terms of the effects that these environmental conditions have on the social relations, culture, social support systems, and other group attachments of individuals living in cities.

Michelson sees the choices that individuals make as being governed by the demands of their life styles. These are in turn a function of their economic state, ethnicity, or life-cycle stage. Again, in contrast with the ecologists, the environment is not seen to determine the types of life styles that individual groups can achieve. Rather the characteristics of the individuals lead to a demand for certain life styles which are then matched to opportunities in the environment.

Residential Mobility as Residential Choice

Michelson (1977a) illustrates this perspective in research that he undertook in Toronto. He examined the bases on which people choose new homes. The people selected in the study had already decided to move and had exercised their options in the choice of homes. Michelson examined these people over a period of five years to find out how the environments that they moved to and the subsequent moves that they made, met their expectations and their needs. He studied the extent to which the environment (in this case the environment included the house type, its location, size, and density) provided opportunity to live a certain life style.

Michelson set out to answer the following questions. First, does the environment preclude desired contacts or activities? Second, does the environment provide realistic opportunity for the pursuit of desired contacts or activities? Third, does the environment provide opportunities to avoid undesired contacts or activities? Fourth, does the environment preclude undesired contacts or activities (Michelson, 1977a:28)? Only by examining the differential ways in which people adapt to their environments after having moved to a new home is a true picture of the congruence between preferences, needs, and environmental conditions possible.

Michelson investigated the differences in life styles (including social interaction with friends, neighbours, and relatives) of people living in four different types of dwellings in Toronto. The four physical environments included single-family dwellings downtown; high-rise dwellings downtown; single-family homes in the suburbs; and high-rise apartments in the suburbs. Michelson (1977a:172-180) found some marked differences between these four types of environments in terms of the types of people that they attract.

In downtown apartments, families tend to be younger. They are generally without children. Both husbands and wives are at early stages of their respective careers. Occupation is more important than are social relationships. With two incomes, this group tends to be relatively affluent. However, with little need for a car, they are heavy users of public transit. Members of this group are most likely to want to move again, preferably into a house of their own. This transiency will also affect their social relationships.

In contrast, the husband moving into a downtown house is older and further along with his career. In three of four cases, his wife does not work. A major reason for the move to this dwelling is its favourable location with respect to work downtown. Again, social relationships are not paramount.

Suburban apartments tend to be larger, with more bedrooms than those found downtown. This choice of location is often made in anticipation that these units will satisfy needs for a greater amount of space. However, the choice of suburban apartments is generally made over such alternatives as older low-rise housing in more central areas of the city. This is done on the rationale that suburban neighbourhoods are more suitable for raising children. Social relationships are thus quite important and are valued by this group.

Families who move to downtown houses put priority on locational requirements. Those who move to suburban houses are more concerned with the house itself and the characteristics of their neighbours. The status-enhancing quality of the suburban single-family home is emphasized by the fact that most persons buying these houses were previously homeowners in the suburbs. The new dwelling is usually larger and in a more socially desirable neighbourhood. Housewives moving into these houses expect more housework, more entertaining, and less easy access to shops and recreational facilities (Michelson, 1977a: 175-6).

Michelson's model argues that social factors lead to a choice of physical environments. These may then affect social relationships. Michelson concludes that we must examine individual experiences (i.e., what people value), if we wish to explain city life. Social relationships are affected by choices that people make in their residential environments.

Data collected from a cross-section of Edmonton households support this argument. Differences in social relations (i.e. contact with friends, relatives and neighbours) do emerge with variations in house type, urban versus suburban locations, and dwelling size. Regardless of the homogeneity of the social characteristics of individuals such as age or income, the physical environment does play a role in affecting contact with neighbours and relatives (Kennedy, 1978). Stokes (1982) reports similar variations in social relations across inner-city, suburban, and small town populations in the Edmonton region.

Restricted Choice

We have dealt with situations where people are able to choose their environments, to a degree, because of high economic status and greater social mobility. What happens when this choice is restricted in lower-income groups? Harms (1972) argues that the market forces which provide choice for middle- and upper-income residents cannot provide adequate housing for the low-income groups in our society. This job falls to government, as a result. It is government that provides public housing to meet the needs of the poor. In entering into public housing, however, the degree of choice to the tenant diminishes. The housing agency selects the location and the house type that it feels most adequately meet the needs of the tenant. In this situation, while shelter needs may be met, problems may arise because of the occupant's feeling of powerlessness in choosing a suitable home. As a person's involvement in relocation decisions decreases while the opportunity to select among alternatives diminishes, feelings of resentment and impotence will increase. This will impair any sense of personal commitment to making a satisfactory adaptation (Hartman, 1963).

This view is tempered by the fact that there are really two different types of tenants who end up in public housing. From research done on Regent's Park public housing in Toronto, it is evident that there are people who go into public housing who expect to stay there. These include the single-parent families with few resources to move into the private market, the very poor, and the elderly. The second type includes those who feel that this is temporary housing and serves as a stepping stone to something better. The Regent's Park study made clear that it is tenants of the second type (which in-

cludes two-parent families) who are least satisfied with public housing when they find that they are unable to attain means to move out
of this market (Kennedy, 1975:205). The rules and regulations of
the public housing environment make life in these areas very restrictive. Increasing choice would be one way of reducing this unhappiness. The political means for forcing greater involvement in decisions about their environments has seen public housing tenants
make some strides in gaining this involvement. We will review this
in greater detail in Chapter 6.

Design for Special Groups

The elements of choice in the environment that are important in
allowing certain types of life styles to develop have been examined
from the point of view of special groups, in addition to the low- income population. Providing suitable environments for women,
children, and ethnic groups, with an awareness of their special
needs, has raised some interesting questions about the removal of
constraints to assist in their better adapting to urban environments
(see Figure 5.1).

Hayden (1980) argues that the conventional home is not designed
in a way that matches the needs of the employed woman and her
family. There are problems of poor transportation. Access to work
and day-care facilities are often non-existent or inadequate. Houses
are often difficult to manage. They require a great deal of time in
cleaning, a task that often falls to the woman. These problems of
poor design often lead to stress in the household from pressures of
time and poor facilities (Michelson, 1980:245). Opportunities for
shopping, picking up children, and so on are further constrained by
poor access and restrictive hours which often follow the nine-to-five
format.

Zeisel (1973) has argued that physical design is often not conducive to the needs of ethnic groups. Architects define space in
terms of its function: bedrooms are for sleeping; dining-rooms are
for eating; kitchens are for cooking; windows are for letting in air
and light; living-rooms are for entertaining; entrances are for coming into and going out of the apartment; playgrounds are for playing; and parking lots are for storing cars. In his study of the Black
and Puerto Rican areas of East Harlem in New York City, Zeisel
(1973:262) reports that windows are used not only for air and light,
but also as observation posts and communication links with people
in the street. Kitchens are not only places to cook and eat in. They
are also places to which older people can go when younger ones are
in the living-room. In the Puerto Rican homes studied, the kitchens
are small. This is a major constraint to the women who value and
are appreciated for the cooking that they prepare. The nonutility of

Figure 5.1 Views of the Neighbourhood

Source: Based on illustration in "What Neighbourhood?" by C. Mercer, 1976. New Society, 35, 694 (Jan. 22): 154-155.

these spaces causes problems for maintaining certain activities in
the home. The problems of small kichens force the women in the
homes to move into the dining-rooms. The men find no space left in
the house. This often results in their leaving the home altogether to
meet with their friends in the relative privacy of clubs and bars. The
opportunities and constraints in the environment, then, can affect
family relations, as well.

There has been considerable interest in the experience of children
in adapting to urban environments. Children live in neighbourhoods which constrain mobility and often do not have compensation
in terms of recreational and leisure activities. The neighbourhood
for them consists of only a few blocks. Even this environment can be
dangerous. Aldrich (1979) relates research in Denver where it was
found that children in poorly designed areas can be very vulnerable
to vehicular accidents. "Child traps" occur where housing is located
on one side of a busy street while a playground area is placed on the
other side. Children who get involved in accidents run out of their
apartments, dart out between parked cars, and get hit by auto-
mobiles. Poor location planning and poor precautions taken for getting children across streets cause problems. Fear of the child's
becoming a victim may cause parents to forbid their children to use
available facilities. This makes the neighbourhood even more con-
fining as there is less choice for activity.

E. CHOICE AND SOCIAL PATHOLOGY: CRIME, POVERTY, AND THE BREAKDOWN OF SOCIAL ORDER

As mentioned above, it is in the effects of the city on social pathology that the contrasts in the choice theories are well illustrated.
Social pathology has been studied, in this tradition, mainly in terms
of social alienation and anomie. The negative effects of being under
psychological stress are seen as having implications for the conduct
of behaviour and for the maintenance of social control.

The Urban Poor and Crime

Two groups defined by Gans (1970:72), the "trapped and the downwardly mobile" and the "deprived," live in the inner city because
they have no other choice. The deprived include the very poor, the
emotionally disturbed or otherwise handicapped, broken families,
and the non-white populations. These urban dwellers must live in
the dilapidated housing and blighted neighbourhoods to which they
are relegated by the housing market. The trapped are people who
stay behind when a neighbourhood is invaded by non-residential
land users or lower-status immigrants because they cannot afford to

move. The deprived and the trapped appear to be affected by the consequences of city size, density, and heterogeneity (Clark, 1978).

The deprived suffer from overcrowding but this, Gans (1970:74) maintains, is the consequence of low income, racial discrimination, and other handicaps. This cannot be considered an inevitable result of the ecological makeup of the city. However, because the deprived have no residential choice, they are also forced to live among neighbours not of their own choosing, whose ways of life may be different and often contradictory to their own.

In areas that are more neighbourly, that is, where there is a high level of interaction between neighbours, there is greater likelihood of informal local control over crime in the streets. In a study done in Edmonton, Hackler, et al. (1974) found that, consistent with Gans' argument, people in lower-class areas ranked as more alienated than those in upper-class areas. Hackler, et al. looked at the issue of the degree to which people in these areas relied on formal intervention in crime through the police versus informal intervention by citizens. They found formal intervention to be greater in alienated areas (Hackler, et al., 1974:341). In other words, communities that are more neighbourly than others prefer informal over formal crime control.

Traditional Values and Social Breakdown

Viewing the problem in a slightly different way, Fischer (1975a) examined the effect of community size and density on measures of social control related to the maintenance of traditional values. Non-adherence to traditional values, or deviance, is operationalized in terms of religiosity, church attendance, drinking, and attitudes towards birth control. In a national American study, Fischer (1975a:430) found that traditionalism is in fact negatively correlated with community size.

Bibby (1980) reports that findings of a national Canadian study indicate that similar trends towards non-adherence to traditional values appear with increases in urbanization. Weekly attendance at church and religious self-image are much lower among urban dwellers than for those people living in rural areas (Bibby, 1980:408). This move away from religious institutions is indicative of an increasing secularization of Canadian society. This involves, inevitably, the development of sets of values which are different from traditional, rural mores.

Density

It has been argued that density can combine with community size to influence crime rates. Booth, et al. (1976) predict that the extensive involuntary interaction that accompanies crowded home and neighbourhood conditions interferes with carrying out the most rudimentary daily activities. Legitimate means for ameliorating these conditions (relocating, mild aggression, and escape) are seldom open to those who reside in crowded neighbourhoods, partly because of their low financial status. In addition, congestion in a community provides greater access to illegitimate means for improving their condition.

Booth, et al. (1976) found, further, that there was greater ease in ameliorating the negative effects of crowding in smaller cities. The opportunity for crime provided by areal crowding is not so great in smaller communities.

Michelson (1975:154) argues that, contrary to the findings of Booth, et al. and others, high density itself is not a determinant of social problems. In a perspective that combines the ideas of Gans and Fischer, Michelson states that the physical and social arrangements of persons at a given density can spell the success or failure of life in that setting. Very high densities can provide the required numbers of persons to support the recreational facilities that many people feel enhance urban life. At the same time, opportunities can exist in these environments to commit crime.

Gillis (1974) argued, along these lines, that treating the relationship between density and behaviour as monocausal creates problems in analysis. Following Michelson, Gillis points out that researchers run a risk when they assume that density produces deviant behaviour. In reality, people exhibiting social pathologies may be the ones attracted to or forced into a high density situation. The high density at this point simply serves as opportunity for crime rather than a determinant of crime (Gillis, 1974:312). Using data from a study of public housing developments in Edmonton, Gillis (1974:311) found that density leads to greater numbers of people receiving social allowance (a measure of dependence). This, in turn, correlates with social pathology (alienation, psychological stress, and juvenile delinquency).

Public Safety

All of these studies indicate a public concern with the consequences of social breakdown in cities. In a survey done in 23 major urban centres across Canada, it was found that crime is the number one concern of most Canadians (Central Mortgage and Housing Corporation, 1979). Fear of crime may be a function not only of actual crime but may be related to confidence expressed in police; concern about newcomers to the city whom people may label as potential criminals; media impressions of crime increases; and personal precautions taken to ensure safety.

Jane Jacobs (1961) believes that safe neighbourhoods are those where there are "eyes on the street," where all people take responsibility for their neighbours and are quick to question suspicious behaviour. Her idea of safe neighbourhoods involves low-rise buildings where people develop a social sense of belonging. With the continued redevelopment of cities, she argues, the loss of street-level contact leads to greater social problems and crime. Some police departments, in fact, have encouraged a sense of belonging through programmes such as "Neighbourhood Watch" and by taking patrolmen out of their cars and putting them back on the beat.

The idea that physical structure affects social relationships, thereby increasing crime, has become a popular one among law enforcement agencies, urban physical planners, and architects. This concept works with the idea that crime can be prevented by creating "defensible space." This can be done by installing good dead-bolt locks or ensuring that windows of houses adjacent to parks face them to enhance surveillance. Oscar Newman (1972) proposes that the physical form of housing developments, when addressed to the needs and life-styles of particular types of residents, can give each group a natural and continuing control of its living area. The purpose of defensible space design is to enable residents to become the critical force in providing their own security. For example, through the redesign of hallways in high-rises residents can monitor the behaviour of people who pass through. As a result, Newman believes, greater security can be achieved. This diminishes the possibility of crime, such as vandalism or burglary. This design change, of course, will make no difference if people do not take advantage of their new-found security.

F. SUMMARY AND CONCLUSIONS

In this chapter we have examined the different ways in which urban researchers have studied the types of social interaction that evolved in cities. The choice model also has as a part of it an evaluative component. Each of the approaches has studied the differences in individual adaptation to urban environments. They have done this through measures of community attachment, social anomie, and assessments of individual quality of life. Differences in social homogeneity, urban size, or environmental design all affect social interaction.

The choice theories include work by Gans, Fischer, and Michelson. Gans argues that social homogeneity does exist in urban neighbourhoods. This brings about social contact within groups where people share common backgrounds. Fischer argues that these groups or "subcultures" thrive in larger size cities where there are greater opportunities for groups to form. Michelson, meanwhile, emphasizes the importance of the physical environment in providing places for people to exercise choice in meeting people and pursuing desired life styles.

The communities that emerge in the city are based on the development of social networks between people. These networks may be spatially based. They form "saved communities." The "liberated" community based on contacts with friends and relatives across the city is more common now in North American cities.

The choice theorists recognize that not everyone has freedom of choice in cities. Those people who are poor or downwardly mobile may be caught in situations that are undesirable to them. It is difficult for them to find adequate housing. They are also more vulnerable to social problems in cities. Choice can also be restricted among other groups, such as women at home, the elderly, or the very young. The design of environments with these groups in mind must form the agenda for future planning in the city.

6 Social Power and the Allocation of Resources

A. SOCIAL POWER AND URBAN SOCIAL CONFLICT

The theoretical perspectives that emphasize the role that allocation plays in cities have taken as their focus the ways in which resources are distributed in urban areas. No longer are we looking at the city as a vast marketplace where the hidden hand of competition sorts out people in space. Nor are we viewing this area as one vast opportunity structure in which people select their optimum environment. Rather, the thrust of this perspective is on the power relationships that exist in cities and the decision-making that allocates resources to various groups. The basic framework in this perspective focusses on constraints, not opportunities. In Pahl's (1969) view, the basic framework of urban sociology is the pattern of constraints which operates differentially in given decision-making contexts. Fundamental life chances are affected by the type and nature of access to facilities and resources. This situation is likely to create conflict.

The basic propositions that Pahl uses in his argument are the following. First, there are fundamental spatial constraints on access to scarce urban resources and facilities. These constraints are generally expressed in terms of time and distance. Second, there are fundamental social constraints on access to scarce urban facilities. These reflect the distribution of power in society. They are illustrated by bureaucratic rules and procedures and by social "gatekeepers" who help to distribute and control urban resources.

Third, populations in different localities vary in their access and opportunities to gain the scarce resources and facilities. Fourth, conflict in the urban system is inevitable. The more the resource or facility is valued by the total population in a given locality or the higher the value and the scarcer the supply in relation to demand, the greater the conflict (Pahl, 1969:147).

Pahl (1969:149) argues that the crucial power brokers are those who control or manipulate scarce resources and facilities. These include property developers, local government officers, social workers, and city councillors. Social problems may or may not have spatial solutions. Decisions by the manipulators of the spatial structure may have unintended consequences on the social structure and vice versa. Pahl states that the current fashion among physical planners for "diversity and choice" implies that differential access to scarce resources and facilities is an independent variable. Rather, Pahl sees such patterns of access as dependent on the allocation by system managers in the urban environment. That is, there is an effect of the administrative rules that these managers work out for the allocation of resources that is evident in the distribution of facilities and people throughout the urban landscape. These decisions ultimately affect this distribution rather than vice versa.

Recent developments in urban social theory have tied resource distribution to aspects of capitalist development. As Sandercock (1979) argues, urban social theory has evolved from social democratic concerns with social inequality and the role of urban planning to a concern with the structural sources of inequality through private and public sector intervention in the urban economy. The work of Castells (1977) is the central focus of this "class" or "political economy" approach to urban research.

Much of this work has used the city as an example of the alleged breakdown of the capitalist system. The focus has changed from the city as a place to live to the city as a product of economic order. The application of theories of the state to the study of cities is important. It suffers from the same problems that were witnessed in the application of social theory to social area analysis, however. The empirical testing of hypotheses is precluded by the inclusion of irrefutable propositions, in this case concerning the nature of class relations in modern society.

In this chapter, our discussion will rest on the dynamics of allocation from a point of view that emphasizes negotiation among interest groups, along the lines of the outline provided by Pahl, discussed above. We will follow the idea of allocation through the research that has been done on citizen participation, planning, and the delivery of municipal services. Up to this point, this research has most often been treated as an example of how the knowledge of urban researchers can be applied in practical terms to solving urban problems. Now, we will be looking at allocation as an integral part of urban research. It is the natural culmination of the influence of bureaucratic decision-making on the ways in which people cope with the city. Comfortable city life is very much dependent on the level of services, including police protection, fire protection, and transit service. It may also depend on strategic decision-making

about the future development and structure of existing neighbourhoods. The delivery of public services and the planning of future
growth are closely intertwined pressures on urban residents. They
determine the degree to which the community remains suitable for
individual needs.

Planning decisions form a major part of the political folklore of
all North American cities. These chronicles begin in earnest with
the urban renewal schemes that were developed to deal with the
"urban problems" of the sixties. We will discuss the problems of
planning in the context of urban renewal and the pressure for citizen participation that evolved from citizen dissatisfaction with decisions being made about neighbourhoods to which they had strong
attachments. We will then turn to the more recent discussion about
the importance of municipal services in making life in cities more
enjoyable. This review will be set in the context of the increasing
complexities of city government and the increased cost of delivering
services which people have come to expect.

B. ALLOCATION OF AUTHORITY: URBAN POLITICAL INSTITUTIONS

In Chapter One, we identified a number of problems related to urban governance. A major difficulty relates to the formal structure of
municipal government and with the authority that it has been given
to collect revenues and deliver services. Under the former British
North America Act of 1867 and the new Canadian constitution of
1981, cities are clearly under the guidance and jurisdiction of the
provinces. Any powers that cities have to finance by direct taxation,
to issue licences, or to borrow money derive from provincial legislation (Higgins, 1977:52). The current practice in most provinces is to
pass a general municipal act which typically specifies: the service
functions that can be performed by municipalities; the structure of
the municipal decision making; terms of office of elected councillors; qualifications for voters and candidates; and the extent of
municipal powers to raise revenue (Higgins, 1977:53-54).

Municipal Expenditures

The relationships between provincial legislatures and municipal
councils have not always been friction-free. A major problem that
arises for municipalities concerns access to sufficient revenue to
provide services and facilities demanded by the public. As Higgins
points out, municipal government in Canada is the level of government that is most limited in sources of revenue that are independent
of other government constraints. The three primary municipal rev-

enue-raising powers are the taxation of property, the issuance of licences and permits, and the levying of fines and other penalties.

The higher the proportion of total revenue that a municipality can raise itself, the greater is its financial independence. The shortfall in revenue must be made up from other sources, ordinarily in the form of conditional grants from provincial governments. The conditional grant structure dictates how municipalities may use the money that they receive. This removes their ability to set their own priorities. Higgins reports that the percentage of total revenue raised by local governments from their own sources has decreased from 62.1 percent in 1950 to 48.9 percent in 1974 (see Table 6.1). This trend appeared, from the figures through 1974, to be headed downwards (Higgins, 1977:67).

Table 6.1.
Total Local Government Revenue, by Source ($ million, and % of total)

	1969		1974	
Source	$	%	$	%
FROM OWN SOURCES				
property taxes	3,019	43.1	4,103	35.9
business taxes	263	3.8	378	3.3
other taxes	37	.5	38	.3
licenses and permits etc.	73	1.0	71	.6
revenue from utilities	331	4.7	722	6.3
investment returns etc.	237	3.4	278	2.4
total own sources	3,955	56.5	5,590	48.9
FROM OTHER SOURCES				
grants in lieu of taxes				
federal government	41	.6	56	.5
provincial government	17	.2	48	.4
federal/provincial enterprises	35	.5	59	.5
other	—	—	41	.4
unconditional grants from province	290	4.1	668	5.9
conditional grants				
federal government	37	.5	125	1.1
provincial government	2,633	37.6	4,841	42.4
total conditional grants	2,670	38.1	4,966	43.5
total revenue	7,006	100.0	11,426	100.0

Source: © 1977 Donald J.H. Higgins. From *Urban Canada — Its Government & Politics.* Reprinted by permission of Gage Publishing Limited. Adapted from *Report of the Tri-Level Task Force on Public Finance* (Toronto, February, 1976), Volume II, Table 10, p. 48.

The problems for municipalities will increase as their tax base continues to shrink against their expenditures. What confounds municipalities in their attempts to avoid greater dependence on higher levels of government is that while their revenues increase slowly, the services for which they are responsible get more and more expensive. In Table 6.2, we can see a detailed breakdown of local government expenditure in Canada. The costs of providing services almost doubled in the five-year period from 1969 to 1974.

Table 6.2.
Total Local Government Expenditure, By Function or Program ($ million, and % of total)

Function or Program	1969		1974	
	$	%	$	%
general government	314	4.2	526	4.3
protection (police, fire etc.)	500	6.7	948	7.8
transportation and communication				
(mainly road transport)	917	12.3	1,649	13.5
health (mainly hospitals)	394	5.3	588	4.8
social services (mainly welfare)	206	2.8	480	3.9
education	3,683	49.4	5,075	41.7
recreation and culture	262	3.5	677	5.6
environment				
water supply	221	3.0	369	3.0
sewage	229	3.1	469	3.8
other	90	1.2	156	1.3
housing	42	.6	166	1.4
financial services	492	6.6	858	7.0
other	103	1.4	226	1.9
total expenditure	7,452	100.0	12,184	100.0

Source: Higgins, D.H. *Urban Canada*. Toronto: Macmillan. Table 2.6; from *Report of the Tri-Level Task Force on Public Finance* (Toronto, February, 1976), Volume II, Table 15, p. 59. Reproduced by permission of the Minister of Supply and Services Canada.

Recent figures indicate that in 1979, local government revenue reached $24,614 million. Of this, locally generated funds — from property taxes, licensing, and other charges — amounted to $12,077 million (compared with $5,590 million in 1974) or 49.1 per cent of total general revenue (Statistics Canada, 1982:3). From these figures own-source revenues have kept up (and increased) as a proportion of total revenues from 1974 to 1979, contrary to initial impressions from the 1969 to 1974 patterns. This means that local taxes have doubled in that time period. At the same time, however, general expenditure of local governments has also doubled in five years (from 1974 to 1979) from $12,184 million to $24,551 million (Statistics Canada, 1982:3).

The fantastic growth of local government has continued unabated over the last ten years, resulting in high labour-related costs. In total, as of June 1982, there were an estimated 304,000 people working for local government across Canada. Wage demands by police, firemen, and other municipal employees have markedly increased the costs of providing services. Taxpayers, confronted with increased property taxes resulting from attempts by municipalities to meet these costs, have begun calling for tax revolts to reduce expenditures on local services.

The tax revolt movement began in the United States with the passing of Proposition 13 in California. This called for drastic cutbacks of the amount of money available to local authorities through property assessments and state aid. The consequence of this decrease in revenue was a reduction in government programmes. Most often, these cutbacks affect the poor and the elderly most directly. When a similar tax bill was passed in Boston, the mayor decided to distribute this cutback differently than in California. He laid off a number of policemen and firemen to make the point that everyone can be affected by cutbacks, not only those who are perceived as having paid less taxes. This strategy brought home the broad-ranging consequences of inadequate municipal revenues to provide needed services.

The Canadian experience with tax revolts has not been nearly as dramatic as the American. Where problems have arisen in municipal financing, the provincial governments have been quick to move in to prevent any major problems. The action on the part of the Quebec government in the aftermath of the staggering Olympic debt was a response to Montreal's problems of generating revenue for paying back the debt. At the same time it ensured that service levels were not grossly affected.

Representation versus Delegation

Municipal government is notorious for its combativeness and rancorous debate. This debate is often nonpartisan, as there is little presence of national political parties on municipal councils. Rather, councils are the forums for independent representatives who, unencumbered by party discipline, make decision-making appear arbitrary. In addition, Canadian cities tend not to be governed through the "strong mayor" system evident in the United States. Mayors in Canada do not have the legal power, for example, to unilaterally appoint civic officials. Often the mayor is no more powerful than the votes that can be won from council. This is true even though the role that this position entails is to act as the chief executive officer of the city (Higgins, 1977:96).

Councils generally are composed of elected officials drawn from wards which divide the city according to population concentration. Questions concerning the role of the councillor and the number of constituents that ideally make up a ward raise a debate over whether these officials should be representatives or delegates to manage the public interests. As representatives, councillors maintain close contact with constituents and gauge their reaction to programmes and services. To be truly successful at this, the council should contain a fairly large number of representatives, speaking for a relatively small number of people. In Winnipeg, 50 councillors represent 11,000 people each in 50 wards. At the same time, in Calgary 13 councillors represent 34,000 people each in six wards.

The shift from representation to delegation entails an emphasis on service management. Since large numbers of policies and decisions are required of council, the decision-making process has to be as streamlined and speedy as possible. By keeping council size down, there is less likelihood of protracted debate and opposing opinion. In this way, council comes to be run more as a consensus-seeking and non-political corporate board of directors than as a politically oriented legislature (Higgins, 1977:99).

The work of municipal councils is very much output oriented and often involves deciding on taxing and spending priorities to meet service needs. It is not evident which of the two forms of government, representation or delegation, best facilitates this task. Clearly, there is a great deal of public dissatisfaction with municipal councils' manner of conducting business. City politics are very close to home. The debates about corporate and physical plans for the city have direct impacts on the public. This is different from the more indirect effects felt as a result of provincial and federal policies. Many councils are populated with members who operate on a part-time basis (since many of them are paid only on a part-time basis). Due to the overwhelming paperwork of managing the city, the debates that occur often miss major concerns. They can focus on minor details that seem easier to handle, such as the placement of a bus stop, rather than on major issues such as overall transit policy. This type of public debate creates a crisis of confidence in the public, however.

The difficulty for councillors is the lack of a political caucus such as gives support for individual members in provincial and federal legislatures, enabling them to divide responsibilities in dealing with different parts of the agenda while agreeing on an overall strategy. The attempt to be everything to everybody has weakened the role of the municipal councillor. In place of political control of cities, the void in managing city affairs has been quickly filled by the city administration.

Municipal Government Structure

Bureaucratic control is not unique to cities. However, the weak political structure in many Canadian cities has left councillors divided

on management strategies and increasingly dependent on policy initiatives from administrations. Higgins identifies four different types
of government structures that operate in Canadian cities.

The "council/committee" structure works on the principle of
council members being appointed to standing committees responsible for such things as parks and recreation, traffic and parking,
public works, and public safety. In addition, there can be any number of temporary special committees to deal with special problems.
Committees consult with the administration, the public and special
interest groups. They then report their decisions back to council.
This structure can be cumbersome and time-consuming in large
governments. In Canada, only one city over 100,000 still had this
system in 1977 (East York). However, it still is the most prevalent
system overall in small Canadian urban centres (Higgins,
1977:108).

The "council/commission" structure is especially prominent in
Western Canadian cities. In this system there is an elected council
and mayor and a council-appointed board of at least two commissioners, with the mayor as a commissioner ex-officio. Each commissioner is put in charge of different aspects of the urban
administration. This can include finance, transportation and utilities, planning, and personnel management. The commissioner
responds to the appropriate committee of council and brings for-
ward to this committee initiatives that need action by council. The
day-to-day running of the city comes under the aegis of the commission board, often run by a chief commissioner. The board of commission is responsible to council as a whole, normally through the
mayor. Department heads are responsible to council through the
appropriate commissioner (Higgins, 1977:113). The advantages of
this structure relate to the efficiency of an executive structure to
manage city affairs. The disadvantages relate to the concentration
of power and influence in the hands of non-elected officials who act
as a screen to council preventing councillors from gaining direct access to the workings of departments.

The "council/board of control" structure resembles the cabinet
form of government. Controllers are directly elected. They form a
type of executive committee. This group formulates recommendations to council. It co-ordinates and supervises departments. It can
also prepare budget estimates for council and nominate appointed
personnel. Recommendations from a board of control can be rejected only by a two-thirds vote of council as a whole (including
votes cast by the mayor and controllers). This form of government
has been especially popular in Ontario and Quebec cities (Higgins,
1977:115). The advantage of this system is again its streamlined
nature for decision-making. Disadvantages relate to the two-tier
level of representatives. Ordinary council members tend to have less

information for decision-making than do controllers. It could be argued that they are representing their constituents less ably as a result.

The final form of government is the "council/manager" structure. In this, council operates as a corporate board of directors. It deals only with matters of policy. The administration, in turn, is left to the government employees under the direction of an appointed manager. The advantage of this system is that council has only one person to deal with in getting their concerns implemented in policy. The problems that arise derive from the concentration of power in the hands of one individual. This form of government is used in Vancouver. It is also popular in smaller and medium-sized towns where the governments are small and the professional expertise of a manager allows efficient delivery of services and programmes.

The formal structure of government, through political institutions, operates to make decisions and implement programmes which affect all aspects of life in cities. Probably the two most important products of this decision-making are physical planning and delivering services to ensure the protection and welfare of urban residents. It is in these two arenas that contact is made with the public and where the conflict about allocation of resources, discussed by Pahl (1969), emerges.

The formal structure of government and politics in Canada is complemented by an informal set of power relationships which operate to influence policy. The role of citizens in planning and decision-making has led to endless debates on the nature of democracy and participation that can be sustained in the city government context. The emergence of citizen power was probably most evident in the struggles that developed in the 1960s and 1970s over strategies for urban renewal of inner cities.

C. ALLOCATION OF POWER: PLANNING AND URBAN RENEWAL

Planning and Zoning By-Laws

Municipalities develop and implement plans which, when translated into zoning by-laws, direct and control urban development. Through provincial legislation, Canadian municipalities must produce general long-range plans. These plans detail the goals of the city and identify principles of land-use, transportation, and service strategies. These principles are translated into a development by-law which directs the administration in the drawing-up of zoning regulations. Zoning laws divide the municipalities into districts. Regulations contained in the laws outline: (1) the use of buildings and land for specified purposes; (2) the maximum density of the population permitted; (3) the height and bulk of buildings and other structures; and (4) the percentage of the lot occupied and the amount of space required (Michelson, 1977b:569).

Where planning runs into difficulty is in the formulation of the initial plans that are translated into development by-laws. Planning has been offered as a rigorous and scientific discipline. The technical aspects of data management and plan formulation set the planners apart from the general public. However, concern has been expressed that the social implications of their work may sometimes be ignored in the need to set down standards for land-use. The ideal plan on paper may ignore the special problems arising from the diversity of population groups in the city affected by these plans. The uniformity demanded by zoning by-laws ignores the dynamics of contrasting human life-styles and choice. When planners are seen as becoming the final arbiters of public taste, confrontation with the public may ensue. Such a conflict arose over the strategies that were developed for urban renewal.

Urban Renewal

Neighbourhoods were treated by ecologists as natural areas where people with similar characteristics live in similar types of dwellings. In contrast, researchers who are more concerned with the values and the socio-cultural relations of urban residents, have treated neighbourhoods as areas where urbanites interact and find mutual support. The social power perspective has focussed on the neighbourhood as an area in which special interests develop and where the power to affect the distribution and allocation of municipal resources is derived.

The early urban renewal schemes initially concentrated on removing "blighted" areas from inner cities. They attempted, through orderly planning, to provide decent, safe, and sanitary housing. Specific factors, such as overcrowding and physical deterioration, were seen to have major negative effects on the social life of the city. "Removing slum areas removes social problems" was the general point of view adopted by this school of thought.

As pointed out above, other urban researchers felt uncomfortable with this simple solution. They argued that such things as differences in age, sex, and social relations which make some people living in slums happier with their environments than others, were being ignored (Gans, 1962). They pointed out that many of the people who were displaced by slum-clearing programmes became very disgruntled with their new, and physically better, environments. They expressed great loss at having to leave their former homes (Fried, 1963). Where they had friends and neighbours that they could rely on in their older neighbourhood, these friends were too far away from their new home to provide support on a day-to-day basis. Thus, although there was a positive change in the physical environment, there was a negative change in the social environment.

Urban renewal strategies date back to work by Le Corbusier in the 1920s. This French architect lamented the reckless disorder with which cities had grown in the years prior to 1920. He argued strongly for planners to adopt a rational planning strategy for the control of future development of cities, which he predicted correctly would grow at an unprecedented rate. He emphasized, above all else, the ideal of physical order (Le Corbusier, 1947).

Le Corbusier's ideas led him to design an ideal city which stressed the creation of highly dense areas, accomplished through the use of high towers surrounded by vast open spaces. These spaces would be interspersed with rapid-transit corridors for quick and efficient passage from one sector of the city to another. The major emphasis of the plan was a demonstration of the possibilities that exist in handling, albeit in a rigid fashion, large concentrations of people in dense settlements in ways that are most efficient for resource utilization and speed of travel (see Figure 6.1). Such a city plan may be contrasted with the old-style streetscapes of areas being renovated in inner-city neighbourhoods of Canadian cities (see Figure 6.2).

Figure 6.1 A Contemporary City

Source: Based on Le Corbusier, *The City of Tomorrow and Its Planning*, Third Edition. London: Architectural Press, 1971, p. 245. Used with compliments from The Architectural Press.

Figure 6.2 Renovated Inner-City Housing

Le Corbusier's ideas received mixed reviews. Many critics felt that his point of view posed serious threats to the preservation of the character of certain existing cities. These, of course, would have to be sacrificed in the overall plan. On the other hand, he found champions in urban renewal advocates who saw his schemes as providing a sense of order to the chaos of existing cities.

Michelson (1977b:575) points out that within the broad concept of urban renewal that developed after Le Corbusier, there were at least two paths of action. The first, and the most commonly used approach, is redevelopment. This involves the developer purchasing properties, demolishing all existing buildings, and rebuilding according to new plans. The second approach involves rehabilitating the existing structures through an injection of capital and resources into an area for the upgrading of buildings and services. There have been a number of urban renewal projects in Canada and the United States since the 1940s. The early projects emphasized redevelopment while the more recent projects reflect a change in public values favouring rehabilitation.

Planning and city politics are the products of compromise. Successes and failures may be differentially interpreted depending on whose interests are being served. But, increasingly, the value of maintaining neighbourhood integrity and community solidarity is paramount to people living in the communities being affected.

Fighting environmental decay (including poor housing conditions and crime) is now often thought of in terms of rehabilitating existing areas while maintaining their unique social and physical character (e.g. Historic Properties in Halifax and Hillhurst-Sunnyside in Calgary). This rehabilitation occurs as an alternative to tearing down existing structures and replacing them with new ones. Social concerns are gaining ascendance, through political action, over physical concerns.

The contrast in approaches to urban renewal between the United States and Canada provides an interesting comparison between the ways in which cities have evolved in these two countries. In the U.S., urban renewal was almost entirely government-financed. Funding came largely from the federal government while planning was done at the local level. Early redevelopment was expensive and its impact on the overall urban area was quite limited. The benefits of these early programmes were not felt by the people living in the areas being renewed. Replacement housing was guaranteed to the people being displaced. These people were generally of lower income, however, while the housing being built in the redeveloped areas consisted of luxury buildings intended to attract more affluent people back into the inner city (Michelson, 1977b:577). The displacement of people from these redeveloped areas, as a result, led to calls for more humane approaches to renewal. These would involve change which did not occur at the expense of the communities of people living in the inner-city areas most affected.

The movement from redevelopment to rehabilitation proved a success, being both cheaper and also less costly in human terms to the people living in these areas. This was so despite the fact that displacement still inevitably occurred as the housing in the newly-renovated areas became more attractive to middle-income families, who pushed up the cost of living there. Even with these successes, however, the overall impact of renewal on improving the structure of inner-city living in American cities has been minimal, as the renewal schemes were too small and too limited. They left many areas still faced with conditions of decay.

The Canadian experience with renewal has been different from the American. It has been mostly sponsored through private resources. The renovation of inner cities through development companies or private resources has led to a major change in the structure of older neighbourhoods in contrast to the American experience. The rehabilitation of older areas of the city has been facilitated by people from higher-income groups who have moved into these areas to invest in upgrading houses.

The consequence of both of these trends has been the dislocation and dispersal of lower-income groups from many of the inner-city neighbourhoods in Canadian cities. Often this dislocation means these people are forced to find housing in less accessible areas. This increases their travel costs to downtown work and facilities. This problem is compounded in many Canadian cities where public housing is generally placed in areas on the outskirts of the city. This makes it difficult for residents to gain easy access to the city.

The advantages of the renewal of Canadian inner cities through the investment of resources in revitalizing neighbourhoods and up-grading structures must be considered in light of the disadvantages of dislocation of lower-income groups forced out by increasing costs and conversion of housing from rental to owner-occupied. Strategies for mixed housing, both private and public, which allow for a com-promise of upgrading while allowing access of lower-income groups to the inner-city facilities must be considered in future developments.

Citizen Power

The negative effects of the programmes of urban renewal on the social lives of urban residents led to their increased political aware-ness. Fraser (1972), in his discussion of the battle over redevelop-ment of Trefann Court, an inner-city, low-income neighbourhood in Toronto, presents a description of the political action that can emerge in an area threatened with development at the expense of present residents. Fraser (1972:263) argues that the most profitable lesson that can be learned from the Trefann Court experience is that conflicting interest groups can contribute usefully to replann-ing their neighbourhood. This "grass roots" approach to planning and urban redevelopment has been advocated in other areas of Canada, as well. In many instances, though, the people in places undergoing redevelopment have organized too late to stop the destruction of their communities. This, in turn, has prompted con-certed action on the part of some social agencies and political groups to provide technical and organizational expertise to the com-munities. This allows them to deal effectively with city hall and with developers who have plans to change their neighbourhoods.

One such project is a booklet published by the Edmonton Social Planning Council. As pointed out in this guide, decisions about neighbourhoods affect people who live there.

> It is of utmost importance that citizens begin to plan their own communities and not merely react to the plans of others. We have remained passive for so long that the idea that we ourselves can determine what our city envir-onment will look like is often surprising. The city may look upon your neighbourhood as one with low priority for improvement or even preservation, but remember

that what makes your neighbourhood important is that
you live there. And whether you are an owner or a tenant,
you have a right to decide what you want your community to be like. Don't wait until a high-rise or a freeway
threatens your backyard. Begin to get together with your
neighbours now and start to formulate a plan for an ideal
community in which you want to live. (Parnell, et al,
n.d.:1).

This rhetoric and the action that followed has led to a dramatic
shift in community politics in Canadian cities. This has had serious
effects on the nature of community and neighbourhood planning.
With major successes for anti-development forces, including block-
ing the Spadina Expressway in Toronto and the Metro Edmonton
Transportation System (METS) in Edmonton, the need for greater
citizen involvement in planning to improve urban neighbourhoods
has been more clearly highlighted. Many "failures" have been encountered along the way, however, as was the case in the battle for
the integrity of Milton Park in Montreal.

Initially, much of the conflict over certain decisions related to urban renewal came as a surprise to many decision-makers. They
began to see the need for a more systematic way to integrate public
opinion into this process, if only to make the implementation of
plans less problematic. The steps taken towards citizen participation have included the development of citizen advisory comittees
and the staging of public meetings on important issues. To some extent the requirement of public hearings has been written into the
planning acts governing cities, to ensure some public input in
decision-making. The success of this participation has depended,
however, on the real power that citizens have been able to wield in
actually influencing a final decision. As Arnstein (1969) argues, citizen participation is another term for citizen power. It is the redistribution of power that enables the have-not citizens who are now
excluded from the political and economic processes, to be
deliberately included.

Arnstein (1969:217) states that there is a critical difference between going through the empty ritual of participation and having
the real power to affect the outcome of the decision-making process.
She developed a typology, "a ladder of citizen participation" which
characterizes the degree of power that citizens actually have in this
process. The ladder includes eight levels: (1) manipulation, (2) therapy, (3) informing, (4) consultation, (5) placation, (6) partnership,
(7) delegated power, and (8) citizen control (see Figure 6.3).

The first two tiers, manipulation and therapy, describe levels of
non-participation. The real objective of these strategies is not to
allow people to participate in planning or conducting programmes

Figure 6.3   Eight Rungs of a Ladder of Citizen Participation

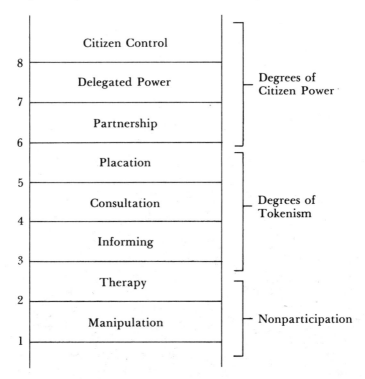

Source: S. Arnstein, 1969. "A Ladder of Citizen Participation." *Journal of the American Institute of Planners*. July. Figure 2. Reprinted with permission from Vol. 35, No. 4, July 1969 issue of *Journal of the American Institute of Planners*, copyright 1969 by the American Institute of Planners (now the American Planning Association), 1313 E. 60th St., Chicago, IL 60637.

but to enable power-holders to "educate" or "cure" the participants. People are made aware of how the planning strategies will benefit them. They have no role in redesigning the plans, however, even if they feel that these do not truly reflect their needs.

The next three levels, informing, consultation, and placation, represent degrees of tokenism. Informing includes relaying to citizens information concerning their rights, responsibilities, and options. Often, this information flow is one-way, with no channel for feedback and no power for negotiation. The most frequent tools used in this communication are the news media, pamphlets, posters, and replies to inquiries. Public meetings have also been used as a way of simply informing people of what the decision is without providing any meaningful way to feed back reactions to the plan.

As Arnstein points out, inviting citizens' opinions through consultation can be a legitimate step towards full participation. However, if consultation is not combined with other modes of participation, this rung of the ladder may be a sham as there is no assurance given that the ideas and concerns raised by citizens will be taken into account in making the final decision. The most frequently used methods of obtaining this feedback through consultation are attitude surveys, neighbourhood meetings, and public hearings.

Placation is still considered by Arnstein as tokenism even though citizens at this stage begin to have some influence. Placation can include the election of community representatives to public boards to speak on behalf of a citizen constituency. The degree to which citizens are actually placated depends on the quality of technical assistance they have in articulating their priorities and the extent to which the community has been organized to press for these priorities.

The final three rungs on the ladder indicate degrees of citizen power: partnership, delegated power, and citizen control. At the level of partnership, power is redistributed through negotiation between citizens and powerholders. These two groups agree to share planning and decision-making responsibilities through such structures as joint policy boards, planning committees, and mechanisms for resolving impasses. Most importantly, after the ground rules have been established through some form of give and take, they are not subject to unilateral change. As Arnstein emphasizes, partnership can work most effectively when there is an organized power-base in the community to which the citizen leaders are accountable; when the citizens' group has the financial resources to pay its leaders honoraria for their efforts; and when the group has the resources to hire (and fire) its own technicians, lawyers, and community organizers. With these ingredients, citizens have some genuine bargaining influence over the outcome of the plan.

Delegated power evolves when citizens actually control the decision-making mechanism and are accountable for the programme. To resolve differences, public officials must initiate bargaining rather than respond to pressure from the groups affected by their decisions.

Finally, citizen control guarantees citizens the right to govern a programme or an institution. They are put fully in charge of policy and managerial aspects. It is they who negotiate the conditions under which "outsiders" may change these aspects.

While Arnstein clearly advocates the position of direct citizen control over decisions that affect them, she does list a number of problems that may occur as a result of this control. Included in these are the problems of increased costs and inefficiency, the encouragement of opportunism among certain groups in getting access to a disproportional amount of resources, and the discouragement of professional decision-making in planning and allocating resources.

While acknowledging the problems of apathy and alienation of the public from the civic government, Chekki (1979) argues that a new experiment in Winnipeg is designed to promote citizen involvement and remove the obstacles to citizen power in decisions about their environments. Under the City of Winnipeg Act, "Unicity" was created, bringing together in a unified government the thirteen cities formerly operating as a metropolitan government. The new form of government was designed to give greater citizen access to the political process, thus encouraging greater "grass roots" participation.

According to Chekki, the most important elements of the new government are the Community Committees and the Residents' Advisory Groups (RAG). The former consist of councillors representing wards of a given community. There are 13 communities, each containing 3 or 4 wards for a total of 50 wards. This translates into one representative for every 10,000 to 11,000 people. The Residents' Advisory Groups contain members elected at an annual community conference by the residents of the community present at the meeting. These RAG members then serve as members of committees to advise the elected councillors.

Essentially, by creating a fourth level of government, at the neighbourhood level, it was expected that community cohesiveness and awareness would be strengthened. The citizen would feel that there was greater access to the municipal government process through local representatives. The Community Committees' responsibilities include the development and implementation of techniques to maintain closer communication between the public and the city government. In this way, residents' views of policies, programmes, budgets, and the delivery of services can be incorporated into public debate. In addition, these committees were to serve an educational role in bringing the public up-to-date on activities by the city that affected them and their community. The RAGs would be the medium of communication. They would be the local communities' forum for getting across local concerns.

Despite the great expectations, when put into practice this Act did not work as intended (Chekki, 1979:38). The RAGs felt that they were being ignored or rejected by the Community Committees. The Community Committees, in turn, felt that the RAGs represented small special interest groups and superimposed their own views on the Community Committees. On top of this, both groups felt that they did not have sufficient power at the neighbourhood level. Despite the Community Committees' responsibilities for the delivery of services in a manner which best responded to the needs of each community, they have failed to play any significant role in service delivery (Chekki, 1979:38).

In fact, Chekki points out that the new local government scheme is not aimed at participation of people in exercising power, making plans, and implementing programmes. Rather its role is to provide heightened consultation, closer contact, and ready access of people to their representatives. Part of the problem which moved this community participation process down Arnstein's ladder included lack of technical expertise, problems of co-ordination across neighbourhoods, and insufficient political power to enact changes in plans and programmes. Also, the domination of RAGs by special interest groups lessened their credibility and effectiveness.

The pitfalls of legislating citizen participation are evident in the Winnipeg experiment. As Chekki (1979:39) argues, the essential quality of citizen participation is spontaneity. It cannot be legislated. To impose participation by law changes it into coercion. However, the structures have to be available to allow the spontaneity to emerge. Critical to this success, though, is the degree of power, expertise, and commitment that people bring to the participation process. The consultation process becomes a process of direction only when these factors are incorporated into the decision-making process.

Looking at the issue of power in a situation where there is less focus yet where decisions are made which affect individuals, we find that such groups as the police, social workers, and others retain certain discretion in their day-to-day work. They have been characterized in this context as "street level bureaucrats," interpreting the rules according to the particular problems being faced on the street. This leads to differing views of the role that these people play in controlling the lives of the people they are serving. Often the problems of the directions set in the organization preclude getting people more involved in making decisions about programmes or policies of these organizations. In fact, in research performed on social welfare agencies in Toronto, Tucker (1980) found that the centralized co-ordination of these agencies effectively negated any attempts that could be made to encourage citizen participation through involvement in formal structures such as advisory councils or boards.

The varied experience of people involved in influencing municipal decisions may be reflected in a distinction that is made between the policies and programmes of the administration of services. While people are concerned about the direction of policy in planning, crime control, and social welfare, they feel that the details of programmes can be effectively left to the managers to work out. The importance of achieving consensus on the overall goals and having sufficient public input into this process will be pursued in greater detail in the next chapter.

D. ALLOCATION OF SERVICES: SAFETY, WELFARE AND OTHER URBAN OUTCOMES

When we talk about the quality of life in major cities, we include in this discussion the types of services that people can expect to receive to ensure this quality. These services are provided by municipal governments to guarantee safety from crime and fire, to provide help to the socially disadvantaged, and to transport people through the city. The distribution of these services has become a topic of some recent debate. This debate revolves around the criteria that are used to decide how these services are best allocated, who deserves or needs them the most, and who is going to pay for them.

The issue of the equality of urban service distributions, it is argued by Rich (1979), is very much an issue of determining what types of outcomes are desired as a result of the existing service. In other words, how effective are local services in meeting the needs of different groups? Are these services allocated so as to produce equal results for these groups? Rich claims that past research suggests that there is a rough equality of services among neighbourhoods. However, this equality is less the product of political choice than a result of decisions made by city bureaucrats to simplify their tasks. Lineberry (1977) states further that the influence of service personnel and the rules that they make in allocating services is so great that the power to influence the allocation of public services falls outside the control of even the most powerful community elite, a point made earlier about the role of "gatekeepers."

A strong bureaucratic influence has led research on service allocation to concentrate most attention on the question of government effectiveness in delivering services according to organizational criteria. Were the objectives of the programme met through the proper development of personnel and resources? Was the programme cost-effective? Concern about the outcomes of the programme for its users has only recently become an issue to researchers. Policymakers who are faced with spiraling costs and high consumer demand to deliver services are now concerned about outcomes. These services are to be delivered in a political climate where there is increased resistance to higher taxes and larger government.

Morgan (1979) discusses four urban service goals that summarize the success of management. These are efficiency, effectiveness, responsiveness, and equity. Efficiency and effectiveness relate to management processes. Efficiency means maximizing output from a given amount of input or resources. Efficiency is, in Morgan's (1979:150) terms, a process-oriented concept that assesses how inputs are converted to outputs. It says nothing about the degree to which goals are achieved or citizen reaction to the service provided. Effectiveness is concerned with objectives. It reflects the extent to which goals are being met. It is result-oriented, focussing on how nearly the desired outcome is being fulfilled without regard for cost.

While the concepts of efficiency and effectiveness relate to government performance, the ideas of equity and responsiveness deal with the concern about allocation as it affects the needs and demands of the urban public. Equity is a concept which addresses the measures of outcomes of programmes. Have they been successful in meeting public need, rather than in meeting management criteria (although these two can correspond)? There are three ways of looking at equity, according to Levy, Meltsner, and Wildavsky (1974:16). In the first, "equal opportunity," all people can receive the same level of service. Second, people can desire market equity. In this case, citizens receive services roughly proportional to the amount of taxes that they pay. Third is the assessment of equal results. An agency, under these terms, allocates its resources so that people are in an equal condition after the money is spent.

Applied to the police, equal opportunity requires the agency to spend the same amount of money in patrolling all areas of the city. Market equity allocates money for patrols based on the areas' ability to pay according to taxes. Equal results demands that the areas where there is higher crime get more patrols than areas where the crime levels are lower.

An area of major public debate relates to the concept that low-income and minority groups are systematically deprived in the allocations of scarce resources. The findings of studies done in the United States provide mixed support for this. What is argued by some is that while equal resources are delivered to all parts of the city, these are in fact not equitable. As Rich (1979:146) argues, the equal opportunity perspective adopted by many agencies ignores the fact that services are offered to people in unequal circumstances. To determine people's needs to attain equal results, it is not enough that standard service delivery criteria be adhered to blindly. For example, some Canadian cities have adopted principles whereby everyone has a bus stop within 1,000 feet of their front door. While this assures equal access to transit service, it ignores the fact that people in some areas of town rely more heavily on buses than do people in other areas. As a result, the buses travel through suburban areas where there are two- and three-car families while people who use the bus regularly end up with inadequate service.

Responsiveness is crucial to service equity (Rich, 1979). Responsiveness concerns the degree to which citizens' preferences and demands are met. However, some research suggests that service delivery, at least in big cities, generally is unresponsive to public demands. Large-city service delivery has become regularized and dominated largely by the operation of bureaucratically determined rules, a point made above (Morgan, 1979).

Rich (1979:147) suggests that if this rule-bound unresponsiveness is common, the inequities that exist in urban services may be largely the products of the institutional arrangements through which service delivery is organized. Such a conceptualization of the issue requires, he states, a shift in criteria for judging service delivery. Our concern becomes less with the distribution of services than the distribution of opportunities to influence service delivery. Some citizens are less able to take advantage of participation and this produces unequal amounts of influence across communities. This is parallel to the thinking of Arnstein (1969) in her discussion of citizen participation. It further illustrates the consequences of differential access to the decision-making process.

The question of a "just distribution" of services in urban areas leads to concern about how this allocation is to be judged. Harvey (1973:100) outlines a number of criteria for judging allocation. First, there is "inherent equality" where all individuals have equal claims on benefits irrespective of their contribution. Second, there is "valuation of services in terms of supply and demand," where individuals who command scarce and needed resources have a greater claim than do others. Third, is "need." Individuals have rights to equal levels of benefit which means that there is an unequal allocation according to need. Fourth, there is a judgement based on "merit." In this case, claims may be based on the degree of difficulty to be overcome in contributing to the production of goods or services. Fifth, there are "inherited rights," where individuals have claims according to the property or other rights that have been passed on to them from other generations. Sixth is the "contribution to the common good." Those individuals whose activities benefit most people have a higher claim on services than do those people whose activities benefit few. Seventh, there is "actual productive contribution" where those people who produce more have a greater claim on services and resources. Finally, there are "efforts and sacrifices." Individuals who make a greater effort or incur a greater sacrifice relative to their innate capacity should be rewarded more than others.

These eight criteria are not mutually exclusive but they cover most of the instances whereby decisions may be made regarding allocation of scarce resources. Harvey breaks down the above criteria into need, contribution to common good, and merit. We can examine these three criteria in greater detail as they set out a basis for making judgment about the allocation of services and ways in which it might be improved through a policymaking or planning process.

As Harvey (1973:101) indicates, need is a relative concept. Needs are not constant. Our definition of "need" must take into account the way in which the need arises. Harvey (1973:102) lists nine areas in which needs arise: 1. food; 2. housing; 3. medical care; 4. education; 5. social and environmental services; 6. consumer goods; 7. recreational opportunities; 8. neighbourhood amenities; and 9. transport facilities. It is the task of the planner or policymaker to establish minimum quantities and qualities of resources to meet these needs. These standards vary according to the economic costs of meeting needs and the social costs of not meeting them. The provision of good education may be costly but the consequences of not delivering education will result in the much broader social cost of illiteracy.

Needs can be defined through market demand. This is a technique akin to the competition model of the ecologists who saw people finding areas which they could afford and which therefore met their needs. More recently attention has been paid to "latent demand." This can be assessed, says Harvey (1973:103), through an investigation of "relative deprivation." Individuals are relatively deprived if they do not receive a service; they see other people receiving it; they want it; and they regard it as feasible that they should receive it. We can best measure this relative deprivation or latent demand through a process of surveying the groups who are both receiving and not receiving services. Needs in these cases, then, are assessed in terms of the expectations that people have of what they should be receiving. Also, they are based on what they think others should be getting measured against what they actually receive. This perspective is similar to the one which talks about matching peoples' choices to the services that can be provided.

"Potential demand," on the other hand, looks at planning for the needs of people in the future based on certain trends in their behaviour or changes which may be taking place in the demographic structure.

One way in which these types of demands can be defined is through a process of "co-production" of public services. Whitaker (1980:242) claims that co-production involves three broad types of activities. First, citizens can request assistance from public agents. This entails calling the police in an emergency or using social service agencies for help in family problems. The nature of the requests which arrive at the door of these agencies can define their role in a fashion that is inconsistent with the current job descriptions but which the public sees as an activity in which these agencies need to be involved. For example, police are increasingly called in to solve domestic disputes where there may be no provision for them to act within the law. Many police forces have, as a result, added the role of mediation in these disputes to their training. They are in a position, as a result, to better respond to community needs. Alternatively, services can be made available for which there is no public demand. The criteria of testing out the success of programmes based on use can help determine the level of programmes that should be made available.

Second, citizens can be involved in co-production through providing assistance to public agents. "Neighbourhood Watch" programmes have evolved as a form of assistance to police. Volunteer work in neighbourhood recreation can also constitute a form of co-production when agencies involved in providing programmes have limited resources, especially money for manpower. On the other side, citizen noncompliance can be expensive if a programme is designed to conform to co-production. Whitaker (1980:244) gives the example of attempts by some cities to institute curb-side garbage pick-up for residents accustomed to back-door collection. This curb-side collection allows the city to collect the same amount of garbage per truck in the same time but with a staff reduction of one worker per truck. This results in considerable saving of public funds. However, for the programme to be a success the public must be willing to cooperate.

The third type of activity in co-production involves citizens and agents interacting to adjust to each other's service expectations and actions. Especially in situations where there is a client-agent relation, the mutual adjustment of behaviour is important to get a useful product. The police have developed strategies of "community policing" which consider the views of local community leaders and incorporate their suggestions about police action into day-to-day activities. In especially delicate areas, where there is a great deal of hostility towards the police, this tactic allows the police to cooperate with the local leaders in cooling out problems while still preventing crime. This tactic became a popular way of defusing conflict in the high-tension areas of British inner cities after the 1981 summer riots.

Co-production is important for services that seek to transform the behaviour of the person being served. By overlooking co-production, Whitaker (1980:245) argues, we have been misled into an over-reliance on service agents and on the bureaucratic organization of human services. The need for flexible and responsive services is underlined in this approach. In a specific case, the responsive service must relate to "needs." In more general strategies, there is still a question of how priorities are set in delivering services and making plans.

The distribution of "common good" (or "common bad") focusses on the question of balancing out, on a larger scale, the resources available for service delivery. This relates back to the question of equity. It also includes issues pertaining to the bases by which benefits can be dispersed in an urban environment. For example, a major debate has occurred in many cities relating to urban parks. In

Toronto, with the Toronto Island communities, and in Edmonton, with the river valley communities, there have been arguments about the right of a "select few" to live in parkland areas. City officials claim that residents restrict access by the rest of the people in these cities. The argument used by the residents is that they do not, in fact, interfere with other people using the park areas. Further, by their very presence, they contribute to the common good by making these areas safer through constant surveillance.

Related examples include debates over the destrution of communities to create highways to carry people into the inner city from suburbs; the distribution of truck-routes which impact on neighbourhoods; and the expropriation of farms for the construction of airports. Determining how to distribute positive and negative common goods is becoming a salient problem for planners and politicians in our increasingly complex and congested urban environments. What this strategy does is to institute a judgmental process whereby decisions on individuals' needs may be based on some assessment of merit.

This concept of merit has caused a great number of problems for individuals who are involved in spreading out resources, especially for those people who are unable to compete for resources on their own terms. (Harvey, 1973:106). It is in this area that the allocative process becomes most crucial and most difficult. Harvey argues that there is an ordering to the criteria of need, common good, and merit. If a facility is needed, if it contributes to the common good, then and only then would we be justified in allocating extra resources for its support. For example, if people live on flood plains when they have no need to and if they contribute nothing to the common good by living there, under this principle they ought not to be compensated for damage they may incur by living there. If, however, they are forced by circumstances (such as a lack of alternative choice) to live there then the primary criterion of need may be used to justify compensation. This same thinking applies to groups who have special needs, such as the elderly and the poor especially in the context of housing.

E. ALLOCATION OF HOUSING: GOVERNMENT POLICIES AND PRIVATE ENTERPRISE

In 1968, a Federal Task Force on Housing and Urban Development was established to investigate the problems encountered in providing housing in Canadian cities. The investigation was set in the context of an increasing awareness of the vital role of the city in maintaining and expanding the nation's economic strength. The backdrop for this study was also, in the words of the Task Force, "the increasing recognition registered so forcibly in the seemingly constant television reports of urban unrest in the United States that the city is a living organism equally capable of destruction as of achievement" (Federal Task Force on Housing and Urban Development, 1969:1).

The Task Force discovered that while it appears that the majority of Canadians still dream of owning their own houses, the increased cost of purchase has made this dream unattainable to many. In 1976, only 56 percent of Canada's urban population owned their own home and in cities over 500,000, this figure drops to 48 percent (*Canada Year Book, 1978-79:*610). In addition, there have been decreasing numbers of single-family dwelling units built since 1966 and increases in apartments and duplexes (*Canada Year Book, 1978-79:*609). This constrained economic choice, of course, makes one's life-style choice, as discussed earlier, more difficult.

Some housing researchers have argued that the needs of those at the lower end of the income scales are met through a process of "filtering." In the filtering process, as households become upwardly mobile they move up the scale in terms of housing quality. The houses that they leave when moving, it is argued, come into the hands of those below them on the income ladder. As housing deteriorates, however, it becomes less desirable for the upwardly mobile group. This housing is not always well located for work nor is it always inhabitable. It is not meeting the needs of the lower-income groups. In addition, with the increasing cost of housing and the increased desirability of inner-city housing that was once left to the lower-income groups, the filtering process is no longer working as it is supposed to. Many people are being left out of the homeowner market. Also, many others are finding that renting is becoming increasingly expensive.

Even among homeowners, the increasing costs of mortgages, taxes, and repairs create hardships for many. Figures for Saskatoon in 1974, for example, show that 29 percent of renters and 9 percent of owners paid more than 30 percent of their incomes in shelter costs (Statistics Canada, 1980:205). If housing costs continue to increase, the numbers of people who find it difficult to make ends meet will obviously increase, creating additional serious social problems in many Canadian cities.

One such problem is residential crowding. Crowding generates great dissatisfaction with a home. Studies have linked overcrowding to juvenile delinquency and family breakdown (Mitchell, 1971). Evidence documented in Toronto by Michelson and Garland found that site crowding, (i.e. neighbourhood density) plays a bigger role in increasing personal discontent than does unit or house crowding (Michelson and Garland, 1974). In either case, it would appear that there is support for the belief that overcrowding on the site or in the unit strongly affects the ways in which people adapt to their housing.

A problem directly related to overcrowding is lack of privacy, both within the unit and from influences outside of the home, such as neighbours or passers-by. Naturally, an increase in crowded conditions in a house makes confrontations with other household members more likely. There will be an increase in frustration in one's attempts to find private space. Dennis and Fish (1972), in their analysis of social (public) housing policy in Canada observed that despite the concerns about crowding and privacy, the form of dwelling unit is mainly determined by the economics of building, rather than by user needs. "The user is fit into what can be built" (Dennis and Fish, 1972:7). Economics dictate that physical space and not social issues is the prime concern.

The Federal Task Force advocated more research on the effects of housing on urban residents, more easily accessible mortgage money, and more innovative design of housing. In addition, to reduce the pressure on housing demand in existing cities, they proposed the construction of new towns outside of existing cities along the lines of developments in Britain, Sweden, and the United States. This new town strategy will be examined in Chapter 8. However, more than a decade later, many of the problems identified by the Federal Task Force are still with us.

A major reason for the persistence of these problems is the conflicting roles that governments must play in ensuring that Canadians have adequate housing. They have had tremendous difficulty balancing the issues of need, common good, and merit in their deliberations about housing. For example, governments have been active in urban renewal schemes. They have had to build social housing to take care of people displaced by urban renewal and those who could not afford housing on the private market. At the same time, governments have tried to encourage the private developer by providing mortgage money. Governments, then, have acted as developers, as landlords, and as bankers. As a result, they have been slow coming forth with an integrated policy to ensure Canadians have housing that will meet their needs.

F. ALLOCATION OF PEOPLE: PLANNING AND THE SOCIALLY BALANCED COMMUNITY

Related to the concerns raised about the differential access to housing is the issue of differential access to social opportunities in heterogeneous neighbourhoods. While Gans (1961) has argued that homogeneity is important for the development of social relations, he concedes that communities have many other functions besides sociability. Planning must concern itself with these values. As a result, many planners have advocated the breaking down of barriers based on age or socio-economic status in neighbourhoods and the creation of socially balanced communities.

As Gans (1961:177) explains it, population heterogeneity has been advocated for at least four reasons. First, this heterogeneity gives variety as well as demographic balance to an area and thus enriches the lives of inhabitants. Conversely, homogeneity may stultify an area and deprive people of access to important social resources such as the wisdom of older people for advice and social support.

Second, heterogeneity promotes tolerance of social and cultural differences and thereby reduces conflict between subgroups in the society. Third, heterogeneity provides a broadening educational influence on children by teaching them about the existence of diverse types of people. It also allows them to learn how to get along with these people. Homogeneity is thought to limit children's knowledge of diverse classes, ages, and races and to create problems in interaction between these groups in later years.

Fourth, heterogeneity promotes exposure to alternative life styles. For example, it provides the learning of other ways of life based on class differences which may promote occupational or status mobility in the society. Homogeneity, it is argued, freezes people into present ways of life.

While planners have subscribed to ideas about the values of heterogeneity and have encouraged them through their plans, Gans questions the empirical support for these concepts. He argues, in fact, that the promotion of heterogeneity (a movement that often goes against the choice of people living in the affected areas) may have a number of negative consequences not accounted for in the four rationales listed above.

In terms of social relations, Gans argues that a mixing of all age and class groups is likely to produce at best a polite but cool social climate. The result may be a lack of consensus and intensity of relations necessary for mutual enrichment. What appears to be a vibrant community to the planner, then, may actually be one that is divided by endless bickering and unsettled feuds for the people living in it.

In terms of the encouragement of tolerance, Gans argues that sizeable differences in backgrounds of groups being mixed in neighbourhoods may lead to negative consequences. Heterogeneity is not likely to encourage tolerance under these conditions, he argues. It may, in fact, lead to strong divisions appearing in the relations between the various groups represented in an area. These divisions may result in the inability of a public official or planner to make decisions that satisfy any group in the area without cries of discrimination and unfair treatment.

The implication that people mixed in terms of class can learn new ways of life which will facilitate their upward mobility has been challenged for the paternalistic attitude that it takes towards people. The idea that the middle-class perspective is the one that everyone should aspire to has raised some questions about the over-emphasis placed on these values by professionals working in lower-class neighbourhoods. They see their backgrounds as being the only ones appropriate for coping in today's society.

Gans concludes that complete or near-complete homogeneity is not acceptable, especially for its negative effects on equal access to facilities and resources in the city. At the same time, total heterogeneity is likely to be so uncomfortable that only those who want no social contact with neighbours would wish to live under such conditions. Planners have to consider some compromise that takes advantage of the positive aspects and reduces the negative aspects of both.

Gans states further that the ideal amount and type of heterogeneity can only be guessed at but two general statements can be made about social mix. First, enough homogeneity must be present to allow institutions to function and interest groups to reach workable compromises. Second, enough heterogeneity must be provided in the community so that important facilities and services can be financed and have sufficient clients to make them function. Economic or social ghettos, either for the very rich or the very poor, are thus not desirable. The planner's advocacy of heterogeneity is in part a way of dealing with the problem of unequal access to resources. However, Gans argues that a more direct solution attacks the problems of poverty and ghettoization through a process of social planning. Programmes are developed for raising substandard incomes. Provision is made for greater occupational and educational opportunities.

Keller (1966) lists seven alternatives available to planners which provide compromises between totally mixed communities and totally homogeneous ones. First, one may avoid mixing extreme levels of the social hierarchy in favour of more intermediate levels. The danger with this approach is that the nearer people are in social type, the more competitive and less co-operative they become. Second, one can abandon the idea of mixing unequal groups at the neighbourhood level but mix them at the community level by planning one-class neighbourhoods. Common services and facilities can then be linked to a single community. This is the idea proposed by Gans above.

Third, one can vary block-by-block composition of a population that is fairly homogeneous economically, socially, and culturally. One can thereby arrive at a varied combination of its several elements at the local level. Fourth, one could take a population which is similar in social class and mix it according to ethnic, religious, educational, and cultural characteristics. This appears to happen spontaneously in middle-class suburbs.

Fifth, within limits one could combine individuals of varied social and cultural characteristics who have similar conceptions about neighbouring. People from different backgrounds moving into older neighbourhoods often find that they can easily integrate into a local social network with neighbours who are dissimilar in terms of income, education, and ethnicity. Sixth, since conceptions of neighbouring, sociability, and community participation vary, one might pre-select residents so they would be compatible in these terms. This means that there would be some predisposition on the part of these residents towards heterogeneity. Seventh, one may mix groups who stress the things they have in common with others rather than the ways in which they differ from them. Keller (1966:509) points out that satisfied housing tenants, especially home owners, tend to perceive their neighbourhoods as homogeneous even if they are ethnically and economically fairly diverse. Thus, under certain conditions, mixing home owners of different social backgrounds may be more successful than mixing renters.

The reductions in inequalities that result from these programmes, Gans (1961:176) argues, would have positive consequences for population heterogeneity. At first, greater social and economic equality would result in greater homogeneity of income and education. This homogeneity would then allow people the opportunity to make choices. If more people have the discretionary income and skills to make choices, they will begin to express and implement preferences. This can create a demand for greater diversity in housing, recreation, and many other aspects of life. The planner, then, would simply respond to these needs and desires instead of predetermining them.

More work has to be done in these and other areas of research to identify points of concern and to suggest ways of ameliorating social problems in cities. The research agenda that faces the urban sociologist is a challenging one and will play an important role in determining the future of urban settlements in Canada.

G. SUMMARY AND CONCLUSIONS

Resources are allocated in cities according to the power exercised by special interest groups. This allocation is predicated on conflict between the agencies responsible for distributing goods and the receivers of these goods. Essential to an understanding of the social power perspective is an understanding of the distributive processes in cities.

The formal structure of Canadian cities combines the political and administrative apparatus of government. There are four different local government structures in Canada. These include council and committees; council and commission; council and board of control; and council and city manager. The two most important products of municipal government decision-making are the development of physical plans and the delivery of services to ensure the protection and welfare of urban residents.

The planning role involves the enactment of land-use by-laws. It also includes a proactive approach to environmental improvement. Urban renewal was an attempt to upgrade inner-city areas. The need for creative, human-based planning was underlined by the failures experienced in simple land-use solutions to urban decay. One important product of the urban renewal experience was the demand for greater citizen input into governmental decisions. The search for citizen power and control set many governments the task of developing formal structures to manage citizen input into policy and programme formulation.

The role of planning includes decisions about mixing different types of people in neighbourhoods, a mixture that the ecologists believed did not take place because of the natural processes of segregation. Gans concludes that complete social homogeneity or heterogeneity is unacceptable. People should be encouraged to mix with people who are like them at the neighbourhood level while sharing resources with people who are different from them on a larger community basis.

The decisions about who gets what in cities depend on an assessment of urban outcomes, that is, the intended results of service programmes. Government programmes can be judged on the basis of efficiency, effectiveness, responsiveness, and equity. The equity question revolves around an evaluation of the needs of users, whether they merit resources, and whether the presentation of the services contributes to the common good. These criteria have been dealt with extensively in policing, recreational facilities, and the provision of welfare. They are also useful in understanding the problems faced in the provision of adequate housing in Canadian cities.

7 Evaluating City Life: Quality of Life and Social Impacts

A. URBAN POLICY AND EVALUATION RESEARCH

Urban research has begun to look beyond urban problems to the factors that contribute to an improved quality of life in cities. Quality of life relates to many different parts of one's environment. It depends on achieving basic living standards, as well as meeting people's expectations. It can be affected by disproportionate allocation of resources, by unequal opportunities or by negative impacts of such things as pollution or house decay. The emphasis in this chapter will be on the ways of measuring people's evaluation of their environment and the ways that have been suggested for improving it.

Much has been written about the role of the social scientist in the development of urban social policy. In the previous chapter, we discussed the administrative structures that are available to handle social problems in the city. We are interested here in the contribution that social science can make to the process of developing policy. Does the social scientist's role involve advocacy of a particular policy? Does it include an advisory position which works to guide policymakers based on insights gained from research? Or, does it simply involve activity as a cartographer of events, avoiding any influence on decision-making?

There is a strong argument for the social scientist's responsibility in guiding the policymaker. Guidance can be offered by assessing the implications of statistical findings which translate into political reality. The data that the researcher collects need interpretation, however. The most unfortunate consequence of presenting to politicians or policymakers data which indicate that the public does not clearly understand a programme is that elected officials often dismiss these findings as being of no value. These results, the politi-

133

cians argue, show the public to be ignorant. They feel that people do not understand the problems of government. Therefore, the need for decisions made in the absence of knowledge justifies making decisions in the absence of information.

The distinction between the opinions that people hold and their attitudes is important in this context. While a policy dedicated to address problems of crime prevention may be enough to change people's attitudes (e.g. fear of crime is low), it may not affect their opinions (e.g. the police are not doing enough about crime). The social scientist's job involves showing the policymaker that while police expenditures have been high and include money for crime prevention, their success can be demonstrated through changes in public attitudes. This may be true even if there is no change in public opinion about the police.

Even more complicated is the distinction between attitudes and behaviour. Many people believe that behaviour is the only true measure of social change. They deny the importance of attitudes in affecting this. Guiding the policymakers in understanding the motives behind behaviour is a major task of the urban researcher.

Work on "applied" problems has moved the social sciences into the policy analysis area. Here demands are placed on researchers to identify factors that can be controlled or that affect the nature of social order in cities. The development of broad-ranging social strategies related to population, housing, and security is dependent on research on the success of existing programmes. The demands for broad-ranging indications of social change have created new needs for data.

B. SOCIAL DOCUMENTATION

To determine the efficacy of theoretical perspectives, it is necessary to collect information about the population and their response to different types of social conditions.

Nineteenth century industrial cities were often the location of overcrowded tenements, poor sewage, industrial pollution, high crime rates, and haphazard development. In these cities, the authorities had little information about the population living there. They had little control over the landlords who kept tenants in miserable conditions. The first step towards documenting the numbers and condition of people living in these areas was taken in London by Booth (quoted in Warwick and Lininger, 1975:2). He saw the problems of bringing relief to families trapped in these cities further aggravated by the fact that so little was known about them. The first censuses recorded the high rates of density, squalid environments, and social changes occurring in these areas. With this information, social reformers were able to make definitive statements about the extent of the inner-city problems and identify the need for extensive resources to solve these problems.

What the work by Booth demonstrated was that an important aspect of any proposal for social amelioration is the ability to assess the present state or condition of the community for which a physical or social change is being planned. This requires the use of empirical techniques for the collection and presentation of data. The data most often used in urban social research are collected either through censuses or through sample surveys. There is also a need for administrative data compiled by agencies, which includes expenditures, revenues, and special tabulations of crime rates, and social service use.

All of these data are compiled and presented in a number of forms. These include social indicators, activity and time-budget analysis, social impact assessments, and evaluation research. The interpretation of these data is governed by the theoretical perspective being used.

Censuses are inventories of defined populations within specified areas at particular moments in time (Kalbach and McVey, 1979:7). The census is designed to provide a specific count of the total resident population living within defined geographic boundaries. It is also used to assess demographic, social, and economic changes. In Canada, the federal government carries out a census every ten years which covers the whole country. There is also a smaller, five-year census. Both provide total population counts, but more detailed information on the Canadian population is provided by the ten-year (decennial) census.

To be successful, a census must have four attributes. It must achieve universality by including all residents within a defined territory. It must gather all data simultaneously at one well-defined point in time (in Canada this is designated as midnight, between May 31st and June 1st). It must be regular (every five or ten years). Finally, it must be legitimized by being conducted by an elected government (Kalbach and McVey, 1979:8). Once these factors have been defined, censuses then face problems of accuracy. Errors can be encountered in any of the following areas. There can be problems with coverage, where geographical areas or social groups are missed in the enumeration. There may be problems with the way in which concepts are defined, as in the case of distinguishing between single-and multiple-family housing when some single houses contain basement suites. Errors may arise where data is inaccurately written down by enumerators or pertinent information is missed. Finally, errors can emerge in the processing of the data.

Censuses are important to a country in providing basic counts of population, identifying areas of economic or social problems, and examining changes in the population through migration or immigration. The information from the census provides us with a global picture of the population. Many cities have become involved in yearly censuses which are used to tabulate demand for housing, social services, and other population-based requirements. The appeal of having total counts of the population is offset, however, by their enormous costs and the problem of accuracy. Every question added to a census form beyond the basic head count contributes to an additional enumeration and processing cost. Because of this, censuses tend to collect only rudimentary information. To do any more detailed analysis of factors affecting social change in a population, the researcher must turn to the sample survey.

The sample survey is a study in which information is gathered from a fraction of the population. This sample is chosen in such a way that it represents the whole. Random selection of respondents allows researchers to argue that they have interviewed people who share the views of a wider segment of the population. According to Warwick and Lininger (1975), there are five advantages of the sample survey which make it an attractive alternative to the census. First, the sample survey is less expensive. It covers only a small proportion of the cases handled in a census. It therefore requires a smaller staff. Second, the sample survey permits greater speed in collecting and analyzing data. The management of field staff, the collection of data, and the processing of information can be completed much more quickly.

Third, higher quality of data can be ensured because of the ability to provide more intensive training and careful supervision. Fourth, the higher qualifications and greater training of the sample survey field staff allow greater flexibility in the topics that can be covered. The questionnaires can be designed to explore issues in greater depth with respondents than is possible with census enumerators. Fifth, the sample survey involves fewer respondents and therefore less publicity. In this way there is less of a feeling that an area is being over-studied, as might occur during repeated censuses.

Beyond its greater flexibility, the sample survey contrasts with the census in terms of the types of insights that it provides. The census provides important information on "what" is happening. The data tend to be descriptive. The sample survey can provide analytical information providing explanations of "why" certain behaviour takes place, how it affects others and where it is located (Warwick and Lininger, 1975:15). For example, the census can tell us how many people have arrived in Canada from other countries in a particular time period. A sample survey can tell us why people immigrated, where they located when arriving, and how they coped with the host society. The strength of sample surveys is that they allow us to make the link between the characteristics of people, their attitudes, and their behaviour.

C. SOCIAL TRENDS AND SOCIAL INDICATORS

In making use of the data generated by surveys or censuses, a number of different strategies have evolved. Often these data have been used to solve particular problems, as outlined in the chapters above. The research on residential choice, for example, provided the choice theorists with a basis for better understanding the ways in which people match residential needs and expectations to housing. Much of the research that is done in cities is of the sort that deals with particular problems from selected perspectives. There has been an increased tendency, however, to develop techniques that synthesize this information, thus providing a monitor of urban development and change.

The social indicator movement began as an attempt to provide objective and subjective measures of the state of the urban environment. Social indicators have conventionally included administrative data collected by social agencies, such as crime rates, measures of fertility and mobility, measures of mortality, and statistics on family breakdown. The assumption in much of this work is that these measures, when considered together, provide an integrated view of the state of urban life. These objective social indicators have been coupled with work done on subjective social indicators which change the focus of measurement away from aggregate effects of change in the environment, due to such things as fertility adjustments, to the assessment of the environment by individuals themselves. These subjective indicators have been used as a basis for evaluating the social well-being of individuals in cities and their reactions to the way of life that they are leading there.

According to Plessas and Fein (1972), a useful social profile based on social indicators should achieve three objectives. It should be able to set public policy priorities; it should facilitate the evaluation of social programming; and it should enable the research analyst to construct future profiles or scenarios of an area so as to anticipate changes that may have significance for social or physical plans.

The attempt to document the most important factors reflecting the state of living in various urban areas has been driven by the concern that priorities, evaluation, and planning should be based on some realistic assessment of the total situation in urban areas, rather than relying on impressionistic views of what is happening. One such exercise in developing social indicators for Canadian cities was done by the Federal Government. The publication that resulted from this work was entitled *Urban Indicators.*

The aim of this monograph was to provide comparative measures of some aspects of the quality of life in Canadian cities. The indicator approach provides a basis for developing a broad-ranging social comparison of life in different Canadian cities based on the level of "quality" evident in each urban area. As the authors point out, advocates of this approach believe that the descriptions provided by indicators may be used to understand cities as they are, as a prerequisite to determining what cities should be. This implies, then, that there are a number of potential uses of these data. They could help in monitoring conditions over time in order to identify improvement or deterioration of different aspects of urban life. They could be used to identify problems that characterize specific cities. They could stimulate continuing discussion on the objectives of society and acceptable rates of progress towards the objectives. They could also stimulate a search for more appropriate indicators and more useful ways of interpreting existing ones (Stewart, et al., 1975:3).

The indicators that were used in this compendium were selected on the basis of comprehensiveness, availability of data, accuracy, validity, and topicality. The areas of concern include demographic

Figure 7.1   Population Turnover

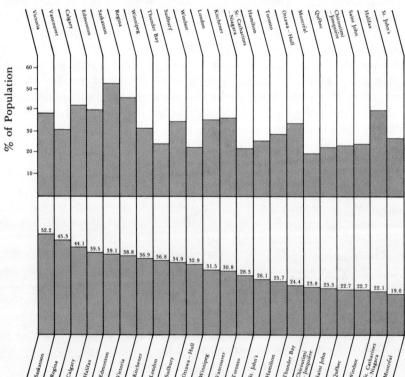

Source: Based on J. Stewart, *Urban Indicators*. Ottawa: Ministry of State for Urban Affairs, 1976, p. 37.
Reproduced by permission of the Minister of Supply and Services Canada.

characteristics, recreation, criminality, education, cultural opportunity, health, income, employment, housing, air quality, and
transportation. The example presented in Figure 7.1 shows the
comparative rates of population turnover in 22 of Canada's CMAs.
This indicator is based on the extent to which there is a flow of
migrants to and from each CMA. It reflects the degree of disruption
in social relationships caused by moving. It also says something
about overall population stability in a city. In the figure, we can see
that the level of population change is higher in Western Canadian
cities, on average, than in the East. This may lead us to ask further
questions about the reasons for this change and the impacts that it is
having on the quality of life in these cities.

The indicators provided in this fashion can be applied in a predictive context, as well. In Table 7.1 there is an investigation of the
relationship between the list of 32 urban indicators and the population size and growth rates of 22 Canadian CMAs. The results of this
comparison indicate that the association between perceived urban
problems, as indicated by the 32 measures, and the population size
and growth rates of the cities is not as high as is commonly believed.
Only five indicators have a statistically significant relationship with
size and only two with growth rates. The importance of differences
of city size, as they relate to urban problems, is not supported by
these data.

What these global indicators lack is a measure of individual
response to changing social conditions in urban areas. Consistent
with our discussion above about the differences between attitudes
and behaviour, we need to be able to include both types of data to
provide a complete picture of the characteristics of urban social
change. In an attempt to establish a baseline of individual response
to life in the city, a major study entitled *Citizens' Concerns in Edmonton* was run in the fall of 1979. The objectives of this study
were twofold. They included determining the public's awareness and
understanding of civic issues, as well as trends and priorities as
defined by City Council and by the civic administration. In addition, the study was to provide a forum for the public to define for
themselves the concerns that they felt should be addressed by the
City (Kennedy, 1979).

Three types of information were collected to respond to these
study objectives. Subjective information included attitudes and opinions of respondents. Objective information dealt with the background characteristics of the individuals interviewed. Behavioural
information included patterns of use of municipal services, as well
as data on travel, work, and recreational activities of respondents.
The analysis of this information was based on an assessment by the
respondents of what they viewed as priorities for action relating to

Table 7.1.
The Relationship of the Urban Indicators to the Population Size and Growth Rates of Urban Areas

Urban Indicator	City Size R_s	Significance Level	Growth Rate R_s	Significance Level
1. Number of Juveniles Charged	−.14	.274	−.05	.418
2. Criminal Code Offenses	.01	.480	.17	.225
3. Percent Offenses Cleared	.03	.447	.28	.150
4. Number of Missing Persons	−.21	.175	−.13	.285
5. Illegitimate Births	−.24	.141	−.16	.242
6. Educational Achievement	−.19	.196	−.37	.046
7. Public Cultural Opportunities	.26	.123	.05	.411
8. Public Library Usage	.18	.216	.17	.230
9. Social Opportunities	.08	.377	−.16	.259
10. Percent Living in Province of Birth	−.39	.035	−.48	.012
11. Ethnic Prominence	−.06	.390	.28	.103
12. Number of Major Ethnic Groups	.61	.001	.35	.058
13. Percent Canadian-Born	−.42	.025	−.35	.056
14. Population Turnover	−.17	.223	.41	.031
15. Number of Hospital Beds	−.48	.013	−.30	.091
16. Voter Turnout	−.23	.148	−.37	.046
17. Income (Non-Adjusted)	.51	.008	.40	.031
18. Income (Adjusted for Housing)	.49	.010	.27	.112
19. Occupational Status	.43	.022	.38	.042
20. Female Labour Force Participation	.25	.126	.43	.022
21. Unemployment Rates	−.15	.249	−.36	.051
22. Annual Strike Days Lost	:34	.059	.08	.364
23. Costs, New Single-Detached Dwellings	.31	.081	.47	.014
24. Percent Dwellings Owner-Occupied	−.32	.072	−.19	.197
25. New Housing Per Added Household	−.01	.482	−.46	.017
26. Proportion Apartment Units	.33	.068	−.04	.422
27. Apartment Vacancy Rates	.21	.178	−.01	.486
28. Children in Apartments	.33	.068	.00	.494
29. Public Transit Ridership	.63	.001	.22	.174
30. Air Quality: Particulates	.57	.004	.24	.156
31. Air Quality: SO$_2$	−.06	.415	−.28	.134
32. Hazard Index	.18	.207	.27	.112

NOTE: Only the indicators underlined have statistically significant relationships with city size or growth rate at the .01 level.
Source: Stewart, J. et al. 1975 *Urban Indicators*. Ottawa: Ministry of State for Urban Affairs. Table 6.
Reproduced by permission of the Minister of Supply and Services Canada.

future change in the city. As shown in Table 7.2, crime, transportation, and housing are considered to be the major areas of concern. This indicates a need for further analysis related to factors that may have created these concerns. For example, respondents' evaluation of police services, their use of the police, and their fear of crime can provide a composite picture of the state of adjustment to crime in the city.

Table 7.2.
Priorities for Managing Short-Term Growth in the City of Edmonton

Area of Concern	Percentage*	Rank
Crime	17.7	1
Transportation	14.4	2
Housing (any aspect)	14.2	3
Rapid growth	12.7	4
Taxes	8.5	5
Public utilities (cost)	8.0	6
Recreation	4.7	7
Neighbourhood disintegration	4.4	8
Parkland	3.7	9
Historical preservation	3.6	10
Industrial development	3.3	11
Downtown	2.8	12
Urban renewal	2.6	13
Annexation	1.4	14

* Percentage of weighted average of maximum of five ranked responses per respondent.
Based on 6586 responses. Total different from 100% due to rounding.
Source: *Citizens' Concerns Study*. Population Research Laboratory, The University of Alberta. 1979.

What these data provide is a relative measure of adjustment. It is difficult to judge, in absolute terms, when a situation is "intolerable" or when "too many" people are dissatisfied that something has to be done to solve the problem. This becomes a decision for the policymakers. But they can be guided in their priorities for action by the baseline information provided by studies such as *Citizens' Concerns*.

In St. John, New Brunswick, a group called the Human Development Council has been set up to identify common goals for the community based on existing conditions in that city. This council has identified the need for information that will help answer the questions "Where are we going?" and"How are we going to get there?" It is through the integration of research and community involvement that answers to these questions will become more evident. In Vancouver, the "Goals for Vancouver" project, which we will discuss in more detail in the next chapter, was built on a process of community data collection and subsequent public meetings to identify future community goals. Other cities, such as Winnipeg, are also using these approaches specifically for the development of General Plans for the community. In all cases, there is an assumption that the integration of data related to the characteristics of the population and their responses to existing programmes is vital in generating good plans for better urban environments.

What these indicators provide is some global concept of change in the society. Once the general patterns are identified, we need to focus on smaller area analysis, provided by social impact assessment, to judge the specific effects of demographic, social, economic, or physical changes to a city.

D. SOCIAL IMPACT ASSESSMENT

An important technique that has developed to co-ordinate the activities of planners and researchers is "social impact assessment". Social impact assessment is a product of the increased interest in the effects that large-scale developments (most often resource industries) have on the surrounding and/or supporting communities. It has also been applied to the study of effects of large-scale development in urban areas. Bowles (1981:7) states that the most basic elements of the notion of social impact on a community assume that (1) there is a defined community with more-or-less stable patterns of social behaviour, social relationships, and ways of life; (2) some identifiable intervention (e.g. the construction of a resource project) takes place; (3) this intervention has consequences that produce changes in the pattern of activities, the social relationships, and the ways of life; (4) these changes are different from, or in addition to, those that would have occurred as a consequence of processes already operating in the community.

Social indicators research and social impact assessment both have their roots in the desire to use systematic data about social phenomena in the formulation and implementation of social policy. However, as Bowles argues, there is an important distinction which identifies differences in the thrust of the two traditions. Social indicators research begins with the concept of trends that are occurring in society, with a concern about how they can be monitored and what the appropriate reaction to the trend is. Social impact assessment begins with the anticipation that, as a result of deliberate changes in the environment, certain actions will be forthcoming that will have consequences for social behaviour. Social indicators research is generally reactive to social changes that are occurring, while social impact assessment is proactive with the development of programmes to minimize the negative impacts of major projects (Bowles, 1981:29).

Bowles states further that social impact assessment is an integral part of the planning process, involving three distinguishable types of activities. First, research must be conducted to establish how social factors relate and how they will be changed by the impacting events. In turn, how do these relationships influence the overall planning process? Second, research designed to predict the consequences of impacting projects being considered or planned must be conducted. This involves forecasting how the project will leave the community after it has been put in place. Third, strategies have to be worked out to ameliorate the unwanted consequences of developments that are detected in the assessment process.

An example of how social impact assessment could improve community decision-making is presented by Krueger (1976) in his discussion of the debate that developed over the new Kitchener Market. The removal of the old market and the creation of a brand new shopping complex met stiff resistance from some members of the public. Krueger agrees that there was a serious lack of citizen participation in the early stages of the development. Part of the problem, he argues, derived from apathy and lack of organized opposition to the scheme. As a result, major planning was replaced with major political agitation, described by Pasternak (1975). Krueger maintains, though, that many changes were incorporated into the plans once the citizens became active and articulated their concerns. What is evident, however, is that the plans for this project did not succeed in incorporating a major social impact assessment to ensure citizen involvement and reduce the disenchantment and unhappiness that revolved around this project. Community reaction replaced community action. Political decisions based on expediency rather than consensus most often result from this process.

E. COMMUNITY DEVELOPMENT

In the sixties the demand for community power evolved into a strategy for community action and community development. This approach is best articulated by Roland Warren (1972) in his book on the community in America, in which he discusses the changes that have taken place over time. He argues for strategies to control the processes of change so as to bring about socially desirable results in communities.

Warren draws from an ecological, as well as a community, perspective. He argues that, despite the lack of formally organized structure, many communities are tightly held together through the operation of informal controls. These are defined by Landecker (quoted in Warren, 1972:168) as including four means of integration. Cultural integration is consistency among cultural standards. Normative integration is agreement between cultural standards and the behaviour of individuals. Communicative integration involves an exchange of meanings, or communication, varying from a high degree of intercommunication to prevalence of barriers to communication within the group. Functional integration involves the degree to which the functions of the members of the group constitute mutual services.

In managing these integrative characteristics of communities, the planner must consider the means by which these factors can be strengthened and mobilized towards the achievement of certain goals. It is through the process of community development that this activity takes place. Warren (1972:310) refers to community development as a process of social action in which the people organize themselves for planning and action. They define their common and individual needs and problems. They make group and individual plans to meet these needs and solve these problems. They execute their plans with a maximum of reliance on community resources. Finally, they supplement these resources when necessary with services and material from governmental and non-governmental agencies outside of the community.

Programmes are developed within the community to strengthen its ability to achieve certain goals. The latter can include the development of community recreational programmes, school programmes, security measures, and informal and formal social support. The inner-city social action groups that emerged in poverty areas in the 1960s were examples of attempts to provide an organizational base upon which local community development could take place. The emphasis in these groups was on the development of a political base which coincided with the important social characteristics of the community. These formal and informal institutions in the community could then be used to achieve certain goals of community restructuring and rebuilding.

In Montreal, for example, groups were formed in areas such as Pointe St. Charles and St. Henri (*Maclean's*, 1981: 16, 18). These were used as vehicles of social action to provide the low-income groups with a voice in dealing with the institutions of government (mainly welfare agencies) and private enterprise. A recent example of how this organization can work to facilitate community needs relates to the decision by a major Canadian bank to close its only branch in the Pointe St. Charles area. This community is characterized by low-income second- and third-generation Irish immigrants mixed with French Canadians. The area is generally poorly serviced by the city. It is surrounded on three sides by highways and on the fourth side by railroad tracks.

The bank announced its intention to close its branch. Faced with the prospect of having to go long distances to cash their cheques or get access to savings, people banded together in protest. They went into the bank and showed their displeasure by opening and closing accounts all through the day, thereby tying up the bank from doing any other business. The bank head office finally got the message and agreed not to close the branch after all. A decision made in the name of bank efficiency would have operated against the interests of the people in this community. It was only through community action that they were able to rectify this problem.

The importance of communities operating to meet local interests is underlined by Warren's (1972:343) concept of the Great Change that he says has taken place throughout North America. He states that communities have moved away from a local or "horizontal" orientation where the control of important community functions lies in the hands of local people. Instead, there has been a development towards community functions operated in a "vertical" fashion. Decision about local communities are now made in central headquarters. They are then passed along to the branch plants or local offices of businesses and government. The problem that arises is an inability to be truly flexible in plans which can meet local needs and can be run by local people. The example of the bank given above is evidence of this problem of vertical integration leading to a detachment of institutions from the communities that they are designed to service. From a community development point of view the sensitivity to local needs is all-important in allowing people to articulate their social concerns. It also allows them to be involved in outlining strategies for the solution of social problems found in these areas.

John Jackson (1975) argues that Warren's approach to communities helps explain conflict that emerges between ethnic groups, as well. His study of a town called Tecumseh, located in Essex county just east of Windsor, indicates that the conflict that emerged between French-Canadian and English-Canadian residents over language rights had its origins in both national and provincial, as well as local, disputes. This cannot be better illustrated than through the example of a confrontation that developed in this area of Essex County over the construction of a French-language school.

The conflict was resolved through the intervention of the provincial government, which overruled the actions of the local school board. The school board had ruled that the French-language school should not be built. The provincial minister of education argued that the first settlers to the county were French and "yet they were deprived of this one thing that they see as a symbol of their heritage and their culture." (*Globe and Mail*, March 10, 1977:5). The minister argued that the provincial government had not acted earlier because they had hoped to change the school board position on this issue. However, they had failed and they wanted to bring the board back into line with the government's position on language rights in Ontario.

What happened in the community was that the horizontal relations deteriorated to the point where strong vertical relations brought about a decision favouring a minority group in the area. What this did for the interaction between the groups at the local level was to remove their power to reach consensus. It left the decision-making in the hands of outside agencies. The autonomy of local communites was thus threatened.

The community development approach recognizes the difficulties experienced in applying uniform strategies to solving urban problems. This is exemplified by the urban renewal schemes. It offers instead the concept that local people should be able to identify and rectify problems using their own resources and their own institutions. When an impasse is reached, however, outside involvement may increase the possibility of resolving the conflict.

The role of vertical organizations in affecting communities was also well illustrated in the relocation of Blacks from Africville to other parts of Halifax in the late 1960s. Africville was a Black enclave in Halifax containing, in the early 1960s, approximately 400 people. It was considered a shack-town occupied by people of low education and low incomes. It provided few services. Clairmont and Magill (1974) report that despite the problems in the area resulting from poverty, there was a strong sense of community. The decay in the area required immediate attention, however. The city responded with a programme of urban renewal which saw the residents relocated to new areas. Africville was then to be redeveloped. Now although the renewal was considered by many to be a progressive step in providing better living environments, there was little or no consultation with the residents about how they would be relocated.

There was some attempt among the residents to respond to decisions being made about them by the City officials. However, there was no co-ordinated community organization on the scale of that which has developed in places like Pointe St. Charles. There was an explicit understanding that there was going to be relocation but the terms and conditions of these changes were not to be influenced by the community.

F. SOCIAL INPUT INTO PHYSICAL PLANNING

The physical planner's role in the development of urban areas has changed rather dramatically in the years since the major urban renewal schemes were initiated. There has been an increased stress on the "decentralization" of planning. Greater involvement of local groups in the planning process has been encouraged because of the greater flexibility it affords the planner in urban design. This approach has not always met with complete success as the planners attempt to juggle local demands with city-wide concerns. One attempt to maintain credibility in planning while maximizing public input revolves around a technique which involves both research and participation in the plan-making. The major focus of this approach is the provision of alternatives, instead of providing the "optimal" plan.

Cutler and Cutler (1976) argue that through a systematic technique of assessment, planning alternatives can emerge that best reflect the conditions that are both desired and desirable to people living in cities. The model for action is presented in Figure 7.2. There are nine tasks to be completed which lead to the implementation of a final action plan.

The first task involves developing a data base inventory which includes a general description of the project planned for an area and a description of the social and physical characteristics of the project area. The second task involves community participation and reaction to the plan.

The third task revolves around documenting existing conditions and analyzing the impacts of the projected conditions under the plan. These relate to urban functions, urban frame, urban fabric, and the quality of life. Urban functions include economic, ecological, and cultural resources at work in the community. Urban frame relates to the nature of land use and circulation of people, goods, facilities, and resources throughout the city. Urban fabric revolves around the character of the urban land use and buildings. Finally, urban quality of life constitutes the synthesis of the frame, functions, and fabric of urban life and their effects on the well- being of individuals and groups in the city.

The fourth task involves establishing the priorities which allow for the evaluation of alternatives. Task five provides for design alternatives based on comparisons of alternative schemes. Task six states the impacts that the project entails. It sets about developing the means to minimize adverse and maximize beneficial effects. Task seven allows for adjustments and alternatives to be considered in establishing the final plan. The last task involves a review and feedback through monitoring of the project as it is implemented.

The simplicity of this model masks the complications involved in matching the social data to the plans. However, the advantages provided by having data available from which to plan far outweigh the disadvantages of planning in a data-free environment. This plan-making provides for an assessment of the needs of a community undergoing change, whether it is a resource community or an inner-city neighbourhood being threatened by high-rise development. The assessment of the negative and positive impacts of projects allows one to accommodate changes in the plan which minimize the problems experienced in implementing the project.

This planning approach casts the planner as a counsel to the public and to the politicians involved in the interaction over alternative plans. It is the product of the interaction that becomes the basis for better plans.

This new emphasis on humanistic planning is reflected in a new

Figure 7.2

The Process: Designing with Environmental Assessment

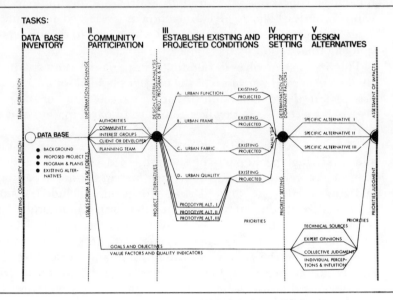

Outline of Component Tasks

Task 1
Data Base Inventory

General description of the project
— History, chronology, and statistical base
— Purpose and design criteria
— Proposed program and plans
Description of project areas
— Physical environment
— Socioeconomic environment

Task II
Community Participation and Reaction

Methods of citizen participation
Information from community
Information to community
Modes
— Hearings and meetings
— Radio/TV/newspaper
— Questionnaires
— Interview
— Workshops
— Others
The appropriate uses, advantages, and disadvantages of various methods and modes — groups reached
Community involvement necessary to discern
— Mutuality of goals and user needs
— Dominant factors
— Priorities of issue
— Alternatives proposed or favored

Task III
Establishing Existing Conditions and Analyzing Impacts of Projected Conditions

Urban Functions
— Existing conditions
— Projected conditions
Urban Frame
— Existing conditions
— Projected conditions
Urban Fabric
— Existing conditions
— Projected conditions
Urban Quality of Life
— Existing conditions
— Projected conditions

Task IV
The Establishing of Priorities Through Value Factors in Order to Evaluate Alternatives

Establishing quality indicators for conditions described above
— Urban design quality indicators (sources of value factors)
— Socioeconomic environment quality indicators (sources of value factors)

Task V
Design Alternatives
Schemes/Projects Alternatives

Presenting, comparing, and evaluating alternative schemes
Project physical program and plan

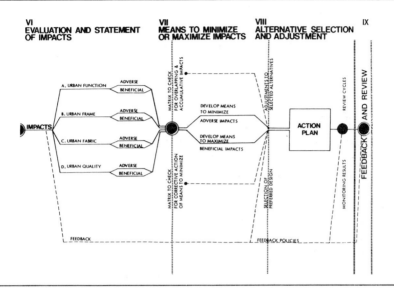

Task VI
Stating Impacts and Developing Means to Minimize Adverse or Maximize Beneficial Effects

Impact areas include:
— Response to goals and objectives
— Responsibility, cooperation, and communication
— Project physical program and plans
— Project operation program and use
— Urban function, frame, and fabric
— Urban quality of life components
Overlapping impacts
Adverse impacts and means to minimize
Beneficial impacts and means to maximize

Task VII
Adjustments and Alternatives to Establish a Final Action Plan

Task VIII
Review and Feedback

Management of assessment and review process
— Assessment — review cycles with agencies and community constituents
— Monitoring interim results — testing by both professional analysis and user review
Feedback into design and funding decisions and stages

Feedback into local environmental inventories, plans, values
— Creation of local environmental base data for future use

Within each simplified Task category the complexity of considerations increases. Just within Task III — Urban Function, Urban Frame, Urban Fabric, and Urban Quality of Life — there are myriad possibilities in describing the components and concerns of a city. Besides, what is an urban frame? Like a living body, the city includes a skeleton or a frame and several separate circulation systems. The city, too, includes a nervous system, which causes various parts to function and behave in particular ways. There is also the flesh or the fabric of a city, and there is the spirit — a quality of life about it that makes it special and individual.

Source: L.J. and S.S. Cutler, *Recycling Cities for People.* Boston: Cahners, 1976, 106-107.

awareness among architects, as well, that what they design should be responsive to the needs and expectations of users. Brolin (1976) and others have criticized modern architects for being so concerned about the visual effects of the buildings that they forget to consider the impact that these structures have on people. Architects have assumed that the public shares their aesthetic values. They have ignored the claims that what they were building were sterile and alienating structures. The large tower blocks in any major Canadian city can be seen as overwhelmingly out of human scale and are surrounded by wide expanses of deserted space. These areas often turn into windy, uninhabitable spaces. Much of this development is offered as symbols of corporate power by the tenants and owners of these structures (more often than not these are banks). The trend to bigger and more imposing towers has left the city dweller dwarfed in a concrete environment with no concession made to human needs.

The response to these alienating structures can include criticisms of the profession that produces them. In this way more innovative approaches in responding to user values and needs may emerge. In the interim, some cities have responded through legal means to restrict the overpowering megablocks. In Toronto, in the mid-1970s, planning controls were brought in that restricted the height of buildings in the downtown core. This attempt at legislating architectural preference led to a greater innovation in high-density design strategies not tried before. The statement of a change in values through a change in laws can have important implications for the way in which the city appears and develops in the future.

This can be demonstrated in other ways. In Edmonton, an architect proposed a plan for an old drive-in site which would allow for single-family homes to be built on a density scale which was much greater than that for surrounding neighbourhoods. This was to be made possible through the use of a lot plan which allowed for less land per house. The architect was challenged on his plan as it contravened the zoning by-laws for the area. He appealed a negative decision by the city's planning department on the basis that this plan was experimental and it provided much-needed housing in the city. The Development Appeal Board still turned him down as it felt that the issues of density and crowding were not adequately dealt with in his submission. The architect did not think to emphasize the social benefits that his plan would generate.

Discussion of this project with the architect made it clear that it was designed in a way that was attempting to maximize the identity of each unit for the owner while still making it affordable. The plans called for different types of exteriors on the houses and varying structures spread throughout to reduce the feeling of congestion. To accommodate the young married couples with children who were expected to live here, the architect planned little play areas close to the house. In addition, the point was made that the development was close to existing playground areas in the neighbourhood which were currently underutilized as the children in the other parts of the neighbourhood were older and did not require these types of facilities. With this type of sociological argument, the architect was able to win his case and received approval for the development. It was the ability to articulate the positive impact that this plan would have on its new residents and those already in the area that enabled him to advance with the project.

G. SUMMARY AND CONCLUSIONS

The social scientist is confronted with the problem of the role to play in providing input into urban policy development. There is a strong argument for the position that the social scientist is the one best able to interpret the results of social data collection to politicians involved in decision-making.

To be successful, the social scientist must have available the tools for collecting information and for applying it. Data collection can involve both census and sample surveys. The strategy chosen depends on the criteria of cost, accuracy, and speed. When the data are collected they can be input directly into solving a particular problem or they can be compiled into a composite model. This can involve either social indicators or social impact assessment. As Bowles points out, social indicators research begins with the concept that trends can be identified in society through constant monitoring. Social impact assessment begins with the anticipation of certain actions coming as a result of deliberate changes in the environment that will have consequences for social behaviour. Both frameworks of social data collection have importance for the development of planning.

Community development, according to Warren, refers to the activity in which people organize themselves for planning and action. The change in North American society from a horizontal to a vertical structure makes local response to social problems more difficult. It also provides a problem for planning communities. The emphasis in physical planning, according to Cutler and Cutler, should rest on developing a sense of local needs and local concerns while matching these to more broadly-based community planning strategies. The call for humanism in all forms of urban design requires greater sensitivity to the impact of plans on individuals in cities.

8 Planning the Urban Future

A. THE FUTURE CITY

What will the Canadian city be like in the year 2001? We can consider the future city in terms of ecology, choice, and allocation.

First of all, we know that cities will be larger. Bourne's (1974) projection indicates an increase of the Canadian population from 21.6 million in 1971 to 31.1 million in the year 2001. Of these numbers, close to 28 million will live in cities (Bourne, 1974:5). Siegel (1974:67-68), basing his estimates on figures from 1971, predicts that Montreal will reach a population of 5.7 million. This compares to an actual number of 2.8 million in 1981. Toronto is projected (again based on 1971 figures) to grow to 5.2 million. This compares to an actual figure of 3 million for Toronto CMA in 1981.

These growth patterns will be affected by factors related to migration patterns within the country influenced by economic changes. The bouyant economic climate in Alberta attracted people to its cities, which grew rapidly. Such population movements can affect the total urban system in the country.

This migration may lead to more homogeneous areas in cities than before. Rural-urban migration and immigration become less important factors in changing these areas. In the mid-1970s a new immigration act was passed by Parliament. This slowed the flow of new Canadians into urban areas. There is more likely to be a shifting of populations across the country from city to city with a more mobile population in search of work. "Going down the road" to find work will become easier than before. As a result of this, will we find that cities become places of loneliness and alienation?

Wellman (1974) gives us reason to be optimistic about the survival of communities in cities. He argues that future communities will be less spatially and more socially based. Innovations in transportation and communication technology will further facilitate contact with people who are alike but who are spatially separated. Wellman found in his research that some intimate community members maintain their social ties primarily by telephone. Either the spatial distances are too great, which discourages continuous personal contact, or people are able to provide support without personal contact. Such ties initiated by personal contact may be maintained by telephone. He underlines that the most important thing is that the intimates are known to be there. They form an important part of the individual's psychological life space, and they can be mobilized in times of need (Wellman, 1974:304).

The advance in video technology will further facilitate the nature of contact with intimates. This advance in communication technology also will have interesting implications for the spatial movement of people to and from work, stores, and shows. In Canada, the development of interactive communication programmes such as Telidon, which works through the home TV, provides new frontiers for social and physical planners to contemplate. It is now possible to work or shop at home. There may be less need to construct major roadways to get people to work or to shopping centres. These may be replaced with transportation facilities needed to carry people to recreation facilities. Recreation will continue to prosper with the increasing numbers of people with more money and free time to spend in these pursuits.

This new technology may also lead to the development of more specialized communities. The capability of maintaining distant contact with people who are the same in terms of background and interests reduces the importance of spatial communities even more. High-density developments containing people of many different backgrounds who have little or nothing to do with one another but who maintain strong ties with people in other parts of the city or country are easy to imagine. The question of choice of communities may increasingly give way to the choice of physical amenities when deciding where to live.

There are some pessimistic views of how cities in the future will be able to manage the resources needed to support large populations. The gradual deterioration of sewer and water works built in late nineteenth century Britain has led to a crisis situation in providing adequate facilities for current large cities. These same problems are being encountered in the rapidly growing cities of Latin America. Canadian cities are facing massive expenses in providing transit services, roadways, sewage facilities, policing and fire services for current populations. The continued growth of cities will further exacerbate the consequences of large-scale growth, which include inadequate services and problems of pollution, transportation, and urban decay.

Various solutions have been proposed for these problems. The large-scale cities of the future, supported by modern technology, are often seen as being able to completely control all of the elements. Buckminster Fuller's domed city envisions a community of one million people living in a contained environment where functional space is pre-designated and climate, temperature, and atmosphere are controlled. This is a plan which is far from being fulfilled. Other designers are closer to realizing their concept of urban Utopia. Walt Disney's dream of a Utopian city has been realized after his death with the completion of Epcot in Florida. The design of this community is to demonstrate how modern technology can produce a self-sufficient complex which includes a mix of people of different racial and ethnic backgrounds.

Paolo Soleri's dream city, Arcosanti, will be located in the Arizona desert. It will contain about 5,000 people living in a 25-storey complex supported by solar energy. It is proposed that each unit in the city will be purchased by residents. These "apartments" would serve as homes, offices, and entertainment centres. People would work in the agricultural activities that provide food for the complex. Transportation around the structure would be facilitated by elevator and escalator. People would have no need for cars.

It is the miniaturization of communities in these megastructures that Soleri sees as a major option available in solving the problems of urban sprawl and congestion. The Arcosanti project is 2 percent completed and starved for money to continue building. The scale of the structure and the need for advanced commitment by people to live in a contained environment such as that proposed may also stop Soleri's plan from being realized (*Globe and Mail,* April 4, 1981:10).

Soleri's proposal for solving urban problems is radical but not completely unlike other suggestions that have been made, albeit without Soleri's technological sophistication. The most prominent idea revolves around the concept of new towns.

B. STARTING FROM SCRATCH: NEW TOWNS

Planners can take the view that starting all over again is the only way to create living environments that are pleasant, healthy, and safe. The most famous of all of these projects was the Garden City plan of Ebenezer Howard. This plan was impressive to so many, in fact, that it still influences much of town planning in Britain and elsewhere.

The basis of Howard's 1898 plan (discussed in Galantay, 1975:55) was that people should be brought back to the land. He believed the contiguity of rural ambience with residential living would lead to a much better environment for people. This plan also had economic sense built into it. Howard argued that the conversion of agricultural land to urban usage raises the land's value. As a result, garden city development companies could be formed to purchase sites and lease plots to people who wanted to build. The conversion of the land would lead to increased value which could then be used by the company to provide needed services and utilities. This would reduce the possibilities of corruption and profiteering which, in Howard's eyes, had such negative effects on existing cities.

The outcome of these plans would be to allow for orderly and healthy growth of towns. People would be close to nature and close to work, thereby fortifying the individual's attachment to the community. These towns were seen as distinctly preferable to large urban concentrations, which were viewed as uncontrollable places of alienation and social breakdown.

In the United States and Britain, in the spirit of Howard, new towns have been constructed as satellites around existing cities. These are seen as a panacea to many of the problems current in the large metropolis. As Galantay (1975:78) argues, decongestion of the large conurbations will remain the dominant problem leading to the creation of numerous satellites and balanced new towns. These new towns will differ from suburbs, which were simply extensions of the larger urban centres. These towns are planned to be self- contained with industry located in close proximity to the residential areas. They become, however, refuges from urban ills and settlements primarily for the privileged. This situation may lead to further decline in inner cities because resources are drained away to assist the new towns. Galantay (1975:79) questions whether or not this money could be better used in renewing existing cities.

Thinking perhaps of failures of the urban renewal experience such as we discussed earlier, Galantay concludes that the money invested in new towns is likely to bring a better return through the development of more housing, jobs, and amenities, than the same sum invested in renewal. The creation of new towns, he argues, also avoids the problem of relocation of people. The problems of land assembly are less problematic than is the case in built-up areas. It is not always possible to tackle the problems of existing cities without stabilizing the population by siphoning off the "overspill" population to new towns. Such relief may be the only way that the historical environments of old towns can be saved from destruction through attempts to adapt the old core to serve the central functions of an ever-larger metropolitan area.

New town developments have been seen as experimental. They act as laboratories where ideas for the restructuring of existing cities can be elaborated upon. Treating the new communities as a chance to begin anew in the development of settlements has provided the opportunity to create environments which are in control and which meet the explicit goals of the planners designing these areas.

In the Canadian experience, new towns have most often appeared as a result of resource development (Lucas, 1971). There has been little experience in Canada with towns which have been built from scratch to contain large numbers of people. One notable attempt to create just such a community was the Ontario government's plans to build a new town as part of the complex surrounding the proposed Pickering airport. Neither the airport nor the new town was subsequently built because of the changing economies of airport travel.

Clarke (1976) argues that there are a number of reasons for developing new communities in Canada. First, the Canadian urban population is likely to double by the year 2000. This increase will require the development of more than 500,000 acres of land. To limit sprawl and the accompanying increases in land prices, new community development will be required. Second, the pressures to apply new technology to communications and the servicing of residential land will be better achieved by starting from scratch rather than superimposing this technology on older centres. Third, there is some limited commitment already by governments to acquire land to decentralize away from major centres. Concern about the concentration of large populations in the three major centres in Canada has led to a demand for a regional planning strategy to reduce pressures on these centres. New environments should be created where control can be placed on population and servicing.

Despite these trends, as pointed out above, there is very limited development of new towns in Canada. Most of it revolves around resource towns, where economic factors dictate the creation of communities in remote areas. The pressures to develop new towns in other parts of the country, close to metropolitan areas, have not grown to the point where there have been many success stories in implementing plans.

A problem which confronts many governments that attempt to relieve big-city problems through new towns is the provision of an adequate economic base to allow them to survive. In the United States and Britain, new towns that have been developed to attract population away from the major urban centres have found financing to be a major difficulty. As Robinson (1976) points out, there was a belief in Britain that large cities were less productive than small communities, and could, therefore, be dispersed with impunity. Small firms in small towns would be at least as efficient as large, specialized industries. That is, there were no economies of scale. It was believed that massive new urban infrastructures could be constructed around the country without diverting resources from other economic activities. On the non-economic side, there was a belief, as well, that people really preferred to live in the countryside rather than in the cities, despite the fact that there were large migrations of people to the cities.

It was felt that the economies of new towns could be enhanced through planning controls, preventing the expansion of industry in unpreferred areas and directing it to areas that were considered more desirable, i.e. the new towns. The planners saw the need to achieve balance in these towns, with the same number of workers living in the towns as there were jobs. Planners assumed that industries would simply submit to the logic of having all of their employees living in the same area and would locate in areas that were away from the municipal centres of trade and commerce.

The final outcome in the British new town experiment was that, to survive, these communities had to become satellites of large urban centres. The small town concept has been abandoned in favour of larger (¼ million) settlements. The idea of starting new towns, with all of the expense of initial capital outlay in building services and facilities, is giving way to the concept of allowing existing small towns to expand. The Utopian view of taking modern society back to the country is too expensive and, often, is not seen as desirable by the people who have to live there.

C. SETTING GOALS: REBUILDING EXISTING CITIES

The promise of new town development does not resolve the problems of dealing with current urban areas. C.I. Jackson (1975) argues that physical planners must have as their ultimate directive the steady improvement of quality of existing urban life. This objective is often implicit but the Planning Department of Vancouver has attempted to articulate it to serve as a basis for planning in that city. The goals required to meet this objective, it is argued, must reflect the basic aspirations and values of the people in the city. The general focus of these goals involves people, change, and environment.

1. *Goals Relating to People.* The city must provide basic resources for shelter, health, and safety. In addition, the city must provide its citizens with access to the widest possible range of amenities and opportunities.

2. *Variety of People.* The city must accommodate a mix of people from virtually every social, economic, ethnic, and educational background. The city must fulfill their needs and aspirations. They must feel that they have a definite place in the city functions.

3. *Variety of Opportunities.* People must be guaranteed the greatest chance for access to occupational, educational, recreational, and

housing opportunities. This must be done without interfering with the rights of other citizens.

4. *Goals Regarding Environment.* All development in the city must be in harmony with the unique features of the city. In Vancouver's case, there should be an attempt to reduce the potential conflicts between the wilderness watershed, the sea, and the urban centre.

5. *Quality of Development.* While maintaining its role as commercial centre for the region, the city must provide a quality mix of commercial, recreational, and residential uses.

6. *Access to Opportunities.* The city must develop information, education, and transportation networks that will allow the citizens to develop and maintain effective communications with one another.

7. *Goals Regarding Change.* Change must be controlled and timed to contribute to problem-solving. It should not destroy the existing quality of the urban environment.

8. *Public Involvement.* In large cities, any change often involves something new at the expense of something old. This leads to a situation that benefits some people, while being costly to others. The public must be made aware of and be encouraged to respond to the costs and benefits of any proposed change that will affect them. Further, a person should be fairly compensated when the costs outweigh the benefits.

9. *Quality of the Natural Environment.* The city must ensure that people within the urban environment are not adversely affected by damaging levels of pollution. (Vancouver, Planning Department, "Shaping the Future," 1974:2-6).

Following this theme, Dakin (1973) argues that a city plan is a product of cultural changes which are reflected in goals for social and physical growth and change. In his discussion of metropolitan planning in Toronto, Dakin (1973:26) expresses the belief that the dominant value in Toronto has been a laissez-faire materialistic utilitarianism. In other words, there is a belief that planning should not impede but facilitate the activities of "good business." It was felt over the years that planning should be rational and responsible. Houses sell better on well-planned subdivisions. Emphasis has been placed on good roads and good services. In the changes that have taken place between the '50s and the '70s, however, the value that "growth is good" has been questioned. For example, good roads should not supplant good neighbours or good communities. The emphasis on functional travel with the construction of highways at the expense of neighbourhoods has shifted and is reflected in the way in which planning takes place.

D. SUMMARY AND CONCLUSIONS

The three perspectives, emphasizing competition, choice, and allocation, that we reviewed in the previous chapters provide us with different ways of looking at the variation in urban development and urban ways of life. These ideas can be compared in terms of the level of analysis that they stress (either individual or institutional); the unit of analysis (social versus physical); processes of change (competition, choice, and allocation); outcomes of these processes (behavioural, attitudinal, and structural); and an evaluation of the perception of the researcher based on his/her values or goals. It must be remembered that while these three perspectives emphasize different factors in analyzing the urban environment, they are not mutually exclusive. They may come together in public policy management and planning, the process through which decisions have to be made about the development of quality social and physical environments.

In the synthesis of these three perspectives, one must evaluate how the links are formed between institutional competition, individual choice, and the concern with public good as it relates to urban governance. We can examine these links in the context of attempts that have been made to co-ordinate planning, design, social control, and social documentation. In each of these areas, the orientation of these perspectives evolves around a holistic approach to urban problem-solving.

We can begin by reviewing different ways in which urban sociologists study the city. These perspectives have ranged from explaining the origins of cities to outlining the ways in which planning and development of cities have come under the influence of special interests in urban neighbourhoods. The increasing complexity of urban environments requires even more research to be done which can help in planning better cities. But does planning mean regimentation above all else?

There are those who will argue that it is exactly the chaos of urban life that makes cities wonderfully unique. These admirers of city life use the adjectives "vibrant," "exciting," "unpredictable," and "colourful" to describe it. It is the sense of place, the argument goes, spiced by a strong taste of diversity, that makes modern cities attractive to many and places them at the centre of contemporary culture.

The dilemma for urban residents is that while urban planning may lead to regimentation, "no plan" always means some inherited or bad plan. As the Goodmans (1947) have pointed out, cities are far from nature, which has an excellent plan. The "unplanned" tends to mean a gridiron laid out for the purposes of economic speculation or, alternatively, a dilapidated downtown where the downtown has actually moved uptown. Planning is vital in encouraging the development of good living environments and equitable allocation of urban resources. But as the Goodmans (1947:10) state, the best defence people can have against planning, and they argue strongly that people do need such a defence, is to become informed about the plan that exists and operates in their lives. They must take the initiative in proposing and supporting reasoned changes that more closely meet their needs and values. They must not be regimented by others' decisions. Our urban future will be decided by the choices made by urban Canadians. They may make the choice to leave planning to others and "vote with their feet" by moving away from undesirable environments. Or, they may decide to get actively involved in creating more liveable urban environments that can be enjoyed in years to come.

The task of urban sociologists is to identify public concerns and choices and to make them widely known. They must communicate their findings back to planners, politicians, and the public to allow them to make informed decisions which would take into account the social consequences of their actions. The urban sociologist must generate a research agenda that will guide work in this field. This agenda should address the following concerns.

Ecological changes will take place in cities due to migration shifts. Also, the residential structures of cities will probably emphasize amenity rather than demographic and cultural choice. The cities will become larger and more densely populated.

The increasingly complicated and densely settled cities may develop in a way that restricts residential choice. Neighbourhoods may become less important as the location of communities. At the same time, the advent of technologically sophisticated communication systems may enhance aspatial communities. The researcher will have to be prepared to compare the evolution of spatial versus aspatial communities. Judgments about the viability of each will present important insights into the problems of social alienation and its cures.

With larger cities come the increasingly complex problems of providing services and amenities to urban populations. If the current political and tax structures remain as they are, many cities will be faced with either cutting back on services or further increasing their already large debts. The latter strategy is clearly a formula for bankruptcy. These problems necessitate research that will contribute to a national urban policy dedicated to the redistribution of economic and political resources to local governments from the provincial and federal levels. Consideration must be given to the restructuring of local political systems and to the increased responsibility, both in taxation and administration, needed by municipalities in order to provide services.

These concerns related to the ecology, the culture, and the political structures of cities are guideposts to further study of cities. They provide an outline for future researchers to appreciate the patterns of the urban kaleidoscope while understanding how these patterns develop and change.

Bibliography

Adams, R.M.
  1960. "The Origin of Cities." *Scientific American*, 203:153-172.
Aldrich, R.A.
  1979. "The Influences of Man-Built Environment on Children and Youth." In W. Michelson, S.V. Levine, and E. Michelson, *The Child in the City: Today and Tomorrow*. Toronto: U of Toronto Pr, pp. 78-88.
Arnstein, Sherry R.
  1969. "A Ladder of Citizen Participation." *Journal of the American Institute of Planners* 35:216-224.
Atwood, Margaret.
  1972. *Surfacing*. Toronto: Paperjacks.
Balakrishnan, T.R.
  1976. "Ethnic Residential Segregation in the Metropolitan Areas of Canada." *Canadian Journal of Sociology* 1:481-498.
Banfield, Edward C.
  1974. *The Unheavenly City Revisited*. Boston:Little.
Bell, Wendell and Marion D. Boat.
  1957. "Urban Neighborhoods and Informal Social Relations." *American Journal of Sociology* 62:414-17.
Berger, Bennett M.
  1972. "Suburbia and the American Dream." In J. Kramer, *North American Suburbs*. Berkeley: Glendessary, pp. 5-18.
Bettison, D.G., J.K. Kenward, and L. Taylor.
  1975. *Urban Affairs in Alberta*. Edmonton: U of Alberta Pr.
Bibby, Reginald.
  1980. "Religion." In R. Hagedorn, *Sociology*. Toronto: HR&W of Canada, pp. 387-428.
Bogue, Donald.
  1959. "Internal Migration." In P.M. Hauser and O.D. Duncan, *The Study of Population*. Chicago: U of Chicago Pr, pp. 486-509.
Booth, Alan, Susan Welch, and David Johnson.
  1976. "Crowding and Urban Crime Rates." *Urban Affairs Quarterly* 3:291-307.

Bourne, Larry S.
   1974. "Introduction" in L.S. Bourne, R.D. MacKinnon, J. Siegel, and
      J.W. Simmons, *Urban Futures for Central Canada: Perspectives
      on Forecasting Urban Growth and Form*. Toronto: U of Toronto
      Pr, pp. 3-22.
Bowles, Roy T.
   1981. *Social Impact Assessment in Small Communities*. Toronto:
      Butterworth.
Breton, Raymond.
   1968. "Institutional Completeness of Ethnic Communities and the
      Personal Relations of Migrants." In B. Blishen, et al., *Canadian
      Society*. Toronto: Macmillan, pp. 77-94.
Brolin, Brent C.
   1976. *The Failure of Modern Architecture*. New York: Van Nostrand
      Reinhold.
Burgess, Ernest W.
   1925. "The Growth of the City." In R.E. Park and R.D. McKenzie, *The
      City*. Chicago: U of Chicago Pr (reprinted 1967), pp. 47-62.
Burke, E.M.
   1968. "Citizen Participation Strategies." *Journal of the American
      Institute of Planners* 34:287-294.
Burnet, J.
   1978. *Next Year Country*. Toronto: U of Toronto Pr.
Canada Year Book.
1978-79. Chapter 14: Housing and Construction. Ottawa: Supply and
      Services.
Castells, Manuel.
   1977. *The Urban Question*. London: Arnold.
Central Mortgage and Housing Corporation.
   1979. *Public Priorities in Urban Canada: A Survey of Community
      Concerns*. Ottawa: C.M.H.C.
Chekki, Donald A.
   1979. "Planning and Citizen Participation in a Canadian City."
      Community Development Journal 14:34-40.
Childe, V. Gordon.
   1970. "The Urban Revolution." In Robert Gutman and David
      Popenoe, *Neighbourhood, City, and Metropolis*. New York:
      Random House, pp. 111-119.
City of Vancouver. Planning Dept.
   1974. *Shaping the Future*. Vancouver: City Planning Dept.
Clairmont, Donald H. and Dennis Magill.
   1974. *Africville*. Toronto: McClelland and Stewart.
Clark, Samuel D.
   1966. *The Suburban Society*. Toronto: U of Toronto Pr.
   1978. *The New Urban Poor*. Toronto: McGraw-Hill Ryerson.
Clarke, S.J.
   1976. "Impediments to the Development of New Communities."
      Contact 8:46-53.

Cohen, Henry.
   1973. "Governing Megacentropolis: The Constraints." In J. Walton
       and D.E. Carns, *Cities in Change.* Boston: Allyn, pp. 454-465.
Cutler, Laurence S. and Sherrie S.
   1976. *Recycling Cities for People: The Urban Design Process.* Boston:
       Cahners.
Dakin, John.
   1973. "The Evaluation of Plans." *Town Planning Review* 44(1):3-30.
Davis, Kingsley.
   1974. "The Urbanization of the Human Population." In C. Tilly, *An
       Urban World.* Boston: Little, pp. 160-178.
Dennis, Michael and Susan Fish.
   1972. *Programmes in Search of a Policy: Low Income Housing in
       Canada.* Toronto: Hakkert.
Dewey, Richard.
   1960. "The   Rural-Urban   Continuum: Real   But   Relatively
       Unimportant." *American Journal of Sociology* 67:60-66.
Dreidger, Leo.
   1978. "Ethnic Boundaries: A Comparison of Two Neighbourhoods."
       Sociology and Social Research 62:193-211.
Duncan, Otis D. and Leo F. Schnore.
   1959. "Cultural, Behavioural, and Ecological Perspectives in the Study
       of   Social   Organization."   *American   Journal   of   Sociology*
       65:132-146.
Farb, Peter.
   1968. *Man's Rise to Civilization as Shown by the Indians of North
       America from Primeval Times to the Coming of the Industrial
       State.* New York: Dutton.
Faris, Robert E.L. and Warren Dunham.
   1939. *Mental Disorders in Urban Areas.* Chicago: U of Chicago Pr.
Federal Task Force on Housing and Urban Development.
   1969. *Final Report.* Ottawa: Queen's Printer.
Felson, Marcus and Lawrence E. Cohen.
   1980. "Human Ecology and Crime: A Routine Activity Approach."
       Human Ecology 8:389-406.
Fischer, Claude S.
   1975a. "The Effects of Urban Life on Traditional Values." *Social
       Forces* 53:420-432.
   1975b. "Toward a Subcultural Theory of Urbanism." *American Journal
       of Sociology* 80:1319-1341.
   1976. *The Urban Experience.* New York: Harcourt Brace Jovanovitch.
   1981. "The Public and Private Worlds of City Life." *American
       Sociological Review* 46:306-316.
Fischer, Claude S. and R.M. Jackson.
   1976. "Suburbs, Networks, and Attitudes." In B. Schwartz, *The
       Changing Face of the Suburbs.* Chicago: U of Chicago Pr, pp.
       279-306.
Fraser, Graham.
   1972. *Fighting Back: Urban Renewal in Trefann Court.* Toronto:
       Hakkert.

Fried, Mark.
   1963. "Grieving for a Lost Home." In Leonard J. Duhl, *The Urban Condition*. New York: Basic, pp. 151-171.
Galantay, Ervin Y.
   1975. *New Towns: Antiquity to the Present*. New York: Braziller.
Gans, Herbert.
   1961. "Planning and Social Life." *Journal of the American Institute of Planners* 27:176-184.
   1962. *The Urban Villagers*. New York: Free Pr.
   1970. "Urbanism and Suburbanism as Ways of Life: A Re-evaluation of Definitions." In Robert Gutman and David Popenoe, *Neighbourhood, City, and Metropolis*. New York: Random House, pp. 70-84.
Garner, Hugh.
   1978. *Cabbagetown*. Toronto: McGraw-Hill Ryerson.
Gartrell, John, Harvey Krahn, and David Sunahara.
   1980. *A Study of Human Adjustment in Fort McMurray. Volume I: Field Study and Results*. Prepared for the Alberta Oil Sands Environmental Research Programme by Thames Group Research and the Population Research Laboratory, University of Alberta. AOSERP Report 112.
Gaylor, H.J.
   1973. "Private Redevelopment in the Inner City." In L. Axworthy and J.M. Gillies, *The City: Canada's Prospects, Canada's Problems*. Toronto: Butterworth, pp. 199-210.
Gertler, Len and Ron Crowley.
   1977. *Changing Canadian Cities*. Toronto: McClelland and Stewart.
Gillis, A. Ronald.
   1974. "Population Density and Social Pathology." *Social Forces* 53:306-314.
   1980. "Urbanization and Urbanism." In Hagedorn, R., *Sociology*. Toronto: HR&W of Canada, pp. 517-548.
Globe and Mail.
   1977. "Ontario Will Force Essex to Build French School." March 10:5.
   1981. "Dreams of an Urban Utopia." April 4:10.
Golant, Steven M.
   1972. *The Residential Location and Spatial Behavior of the Elderly: A Canadian Example*. Department of Geography, Research Paper No. 143. Chicago: University of Chicago.
Gold, Harry.
   1982. *The Sociology of Urban Life*. Englewood Cliffs: Prentice-Hall.
Golden, Hilda H.
   1981. *Urbanization and Cities*. Lexington, Mass.: Heath.
Goodman, Paul and Percival.
   1947. *Communitas*. New York: Vintage (reprinted 1960).
Greer, Scott.
   1956. "Urbanism Reconsidered: A Comparative Study of Local Areas of a Metropolis." *American Sociological Review* 21:19-25.

Guest, Avery.
  1969. "The Applicability of the Burgess Zonal Hypothesis to Urban
    Canada." *Demography* 6:271-7.
Hackler, James, Kwai-Yiu Ho, and Carol Urquhart Ross.
  1974. "The Willingness to Intervene: Differing Community Character-
    istics." *Social Problems* 21:328-344.
Hardwick, Walter G.
  1974. *Vancouver*. Toronto: Collier-Macmillan.
Harms, H.
  1972. "The Housing Problem for Low-Income People." In J.F. Turner,
    Freedom to Build. New York: Macmillan, pp. 73-94.
Harris, Chauncy and Edward L. Ullman.
  1945. "The Nature of Cities." *Annals of the American Academy of
    Political and Social Science,* 242:7-17.
Hartman, Chester.
  1963. "Social Values and Housing Orientations." *Journal of Social
    Issues* 19:113-131.
Harvey, David.
  1973. *Social Justice and the City*. Baltimore: Johns Hopkins U.P.
Hawley, Amos.
  1981. "Human Ecology: Persistence and Change." *American Behav-
    ioural Scientist* 24:423-444.
Hayden, S.
  1980. "What Would a Non-sexist City Be Like?" *Signs* 5:51-70.
Hayner, N.S.
  1968. "Mexico City: Its Growth and Configuration, 1345-1960." In
    Fava, S.F., *Urbanism in World Perspective*. New York: Crowell,
    pp. 166-176.
Higgins, D.J.H.
  1977. *Urban Canada: Its Government and Politics*. Toronto: Macmillan
    of Canada.
Hodge, Gerald and M.A. Qadeer.
  1980. "The Persistence of Canadian Towns and Villages: Small is
    Viable." *Urban Geography,* 1:335-349.
Howard, Ebenezer.
  1898. *Garden Cities of Tomorrow*. London: Faber (reprinted in 1946).
Hoyt, Homer.
  1939. *The Structure and Growth of Urban Areas*. Washington: Federal
    Housing Authority.
Hughes, Everett C.
  1943. *French Canada in Transition*. Chicago: U of Chicago Pr.
Hunter, Alfred A. and A.H. Latif.
  1973. "Stability and Change in the Ecological Structure of Winnipeg: A
    Multi-Method Approach." *Canadian Review of Sociology and
    Anthropology,* 10:308-333.
Jackson, C.I.
  1975. *Canadian Settlements — Perspectives*. Ottawa: Ministry of State
    for Urban Affairs.
Jackson, John D.
  1975. *Community and Conflict*. Toronto: HR&W of Canada.

Jacobs, Jane.
   1961. *The Death and Life of the Great American Cities.* New York:
      Random House.
Kalbach, Warren and Wayne W. McVey.
   1979. *The Demographic Bases of Canadian Society.* Toronto: McGraw-
      Hill Ryerson.
Katz, Michael.
   1969. "Social Structure in Hamilton, Ontario." In S. Thernstrom and
      R. Sennett, *Nineteenth-Century Cities.* New Haven: Yale U Pr,
      pp. 209-244.
Keller, Susanne.
   1966. "Social Class in Physical Planning." *International Social Science
      Journal* 18:494-512.
Kennedy, Leslie W.
   1975. "Residential Mobility as a Cyclical Process." Unpublished PhD
      Thesis, University of Toronto.
   1978. "Environmental Opportunity and Social Contact: A True or
      Spurious Relationship?" *Pacific Sociological Review,* 21:173-186.
   1979. "Citizens' Concerns in Edmonton." *Urban Forum,* 4:32-39.
Kennedy, Leslie W., Clifford Kinzel, and Herbert Northcott.
   1978. *Initial Findings from the 1978 Edmonton Area Study.* Edmonton
      Area Series #7. Edmonton: Population Research Laboratory.
Krueger, R.R.
   1976. "The Kitchener Market Fight: Another View." *Urban Forum*
      2:40-47.
Le Corbusier.
   1947. *The City of Tomorrow.* London: Architectural Pr.
Levy, F.S., J. Meltsner, and A. Wildavsky.
   1974. *Urban Outcomes.* Berkeley: U of Cal Pr.
Lineberry, Robert L.
   1977. *Equality and Urban Policy.* Beverly Hills: Sage.
Long, L.H.
   1980. "Back to the Countryside and Back to the City in the Same
      Decade." In S.B. Laska and D. Spain, *Back to the City: Issues in
      Neighborhood Renovation.* New York: Pergamon. pp. 61-76.
Lucas, Rex.
   1971. *Minetown, Milltown, Railtown.* Toronto: U of Toronto Pr.
McCann, L.D.
   1975. "Neighbourhoods in Transition." Edmonton: University of
      Alberta, Studies in Geography Occasional Papers 2.
McKenzie, Roderick D.
   1926. "The Scope of Human Ecology." In E.W. Burgess, ed. *The Urban
      Community.* Chicago: U of Chicago Pr.
Maclean's.
   1981. "David Triumphs Over Goliath." June 18, pp. 16-18.
McVey, Wayne W., Jr.
   1978. "Migration and the Smaller Community." *Canadian Studies in
      Population* 5:13-23.

Michelson, William.
   1975. *Man and His Urban Environment*. 2nd ed. Reading, Mass.: Addison-Wesley.
   1977a. *Environmental Choice, Human Behavior, and Residential Satisfaction*. New York: Oxford U Pr.
   1977b. "Planning and the Amelioration of Urban Problems." In K.P. Schwirian, *Contemporary Topics in Urban Sociology*. Morristown, N.J.: General Learning Pr, pp. 562-640.
   1980. "Long and Short Range Criteria for Housing Choice and Environmental Behavior." *Journal of Social Issues* 36:135-145.
Michelson, William and Kevin Garland.
   1974. *The Differential Role of Crowded Homes in the Incidence of Selected Symptoms of Social Pathology*. Toronto: Centre for Urban and Community Studies, Research Paper No. 67.
Milgram, Stanley.
   1977. "The Experience of Living in Cities." In J. Walton and D.E. Carns, *Cities in Change*. Boston: Allyn, pp. 101-113.
Mitchell, Robert.
   1971. "Some Social Implications of High Density Housing." *American Sociological Review* 36:18-29.
Morgan, David.
   1979. *Managing Urban America*. North Scituate, Mass.: Duxbury Pr.
Murdie, Robert.
   1969. *Factorial Ecology of Metropolitan Toronto 1951-61*. Chicago: Department of Geography Research Series, University of Chicago, Research Paper #116.
Nader, George A.
   1975. *Cities of Canada*, Vols 1 and 2. Toronto: Macmillan of Canada.
Newman, Oscar.
   1972. *Defensible Space*. New York: Macmillan.
Newsweek.
   1982. "Mexico." July 12 :53.
Pahl, Robert E.
   1969. "Urban Social Theory and Research." *Environment and Planning* 1:143-153.
Park, Robert E.
   1925. "The City: Suggestions for the Investigation of Human Behavior in the Urban Environment." In Robert Park, Ernest Burgess, and Roderick D. McKenzie, *The City*. Chicago: U of Chicago Pr. (reprinted 1967), pp. 1-46.
Parnell, et al.
   n.d. *Rape of the Block*. Edmonton: Edmonton Social Planning Council.
Pasternak, J.
   1975. *The Kitchener Market Fight*. Toronto: Hakkert.
Pawley, M.
   1971. *Architecture Versus Housing*. New York: Praeger.
Pineo, Peter E.
   1966. "The Extended Family in a Working-Class Area of Hamilton." In B. Blishen, et. al. *Canadian Society*. Toronto: Macmillan of Canada, pp. 140-150.

Plessas, Dimitri and Ricca Fein.
  1972. "An Evaluation of Social Indicators." *Journal of the American Institute of Planners* (Jan.) :43-51.
Poplin, Dennis E.
  1979. *Communities.* New York: Macmillan.
Redfield, Robert.
  1953. *The Primitive World and Its Transformations.* Ithaca: Great Seals.
Rich, Richard C.
  1979. "Neglected Issues in the Study of Urban Service Distributions: A Research Agenda." *Urban Studies* 16:143-156.
Richler, Mordecai.
  1969. *The Apprenticeship of Duddy Kravitz.* Toronto: McClelland and Stewart.
Richmond, Anthony H.
  1974. *Aspects of the Absorption and Adaptation of Immigrants.* Ottawa: Information Canada.
Riesman, David.
  1958. "The Suburban Sadness." In W.M. Dobriner, *The Suburban Community.* New York: Putnam, pp. 375-408.
Robinson, A.J.
  1976. "New Communities for Canada: Economic Aspects." *Contact* 8:125-136.
Robinson, W.S.
  1950. "Ecological Correlation and the Behavior of Individuals." *American Sociological Review* 15:351-357.
Sandercock, L.
  1979. "Political Economy and Urban Sociology." *Australian and New Zealand Journal of Sociology* 15:70-73.
Schwirian, Kent P. and M. Matre.
  1974. "The Ecological Structure of Canadian Cities." In K.P. Schwirian, *Comparative Urban Structure: Studies in the Ecology of Cities.* Lexington: Heath, pp. 309-323.
Shevky, Eshref and Wendell Bell.
  1955. *Social Area Analysis: Theory, Illustrative Application, and Computational Procedures.* Stanford: Stanford U Pr.
Shulman, Norman.
  1975. "Life-Cycle Variations in Patterns of Close Relationships." *Journal of Marriage and the Family* 37:813-821.
Siegel, Jay.
  1974. "Forecasting Urban Populations." In L.S. Bourne, R.D. MacKinnon, J. Siegel, and J.W. Simmons, *Urban Futures for Central Canada: Perspectives on Forecasting Urban Growth and Form.* Toronto: U of Toronto Pr, pp. 60-78.
Simmons, James.
  1974. *Patterns of Residential Movement in Metropolitan Toronto.* Toronto: U of Toronto Pr.
Sinclair, Peter R. and Kenneth Westhues.
  1974. *Village in Crisis.* Toronto: HR&W of Canada.

Sjoberg, Gideon.
   1960.   *The Preindustrial City.* New York: Free Pr.
   1970.   "Theory and Research in Urban Sociology." In Robert Gutman and David Popenoe, *Neighborhood, City, and Metropolis.* New York: Random House, pp. 85-108.
Spear, Peter.
   1979.   "Rural Alberta and the Country Residence Owner." In McDonald, M., *Small Town Alberta Proceedings.* Edmonton: University of Alberta Extension Faculty, pp. 8-42.
Statistics Canada.
   1980.   *Perspectives Canada III.* Ottawa: Supply and Services Canada.
   1981.   *1981 Census Pub. #93-909.* Ottawa: Supply and Services Canada.
   1982.   *Infomat,* September 17. Ottawa: Supply and Services Canada.
Stewart, John N., David Belgue, Wayne Bond, Odette L'Anglais and Huguette Turcotte.
   1975.   *Urban Indicators: Quality of Life Comparisons for Canadian Cities.* Ottawa: Ministry of State for Urban Affairs.
Stokes, Dennis.
   1982.   *Determinants of Social Contact.* Unpublished PhD thesis, University of Alberta, Edmonton, Alberta.
Suttles, Gerald.
   1972.   *The Social Construction of Communities.* Chicago: U of Chicago Pr.
Thoreau, H.D.
   1969.   *Walden.* Princeton: Princeton U Pr.
Tilly, Charles.
   1974.   *An Urban World.* Boston: Little.
Toronto Star.
   1974.   "Toronto Crime Rate Twice as High as Scarborough's." March 22:3.
Tucker, D.J.
   1980.   "Coordination and Citizen Participation." *Social Service Review* (March) :13-30.
Turner, F.C.
   1976.   "The Rush to the Cities in Latin America." *Science* 192:955-961.
United Nations.
   1982.   *World Data Sheet.* New York: UNA-USA.
Urban Forum.
   1977.   "Recycling the Inner City: an Alternative to Suburban Development." June: 6-9.
Van Vliet, Willem.
   1979.   "The Community of Urban Sociologists in Canada: An Examination of Spatial Distance, Professional Opinions and Interactional Ties." Toronto: Centre for Urban and Community Studies, Research Paper 105.
Warren, Donald.
   1977.   "Neighborhoods in Urban Areas." In R.L. Warren, *New Perspectives on the American Community.* 3rd ed. Skokie, Ill.: Rand.

Warren, Roland L.
1972. *The Community in America*. Chicago: Rand.
Warwick, Donald and Charles A. Lininger.
1975. *The Sample Survey*. Toronto: McGraw-Hill Ryerson.
Wayne, Jack.
1972. "The Case of the Friendless Urbanite." In Alan Powell, *The City*. Toronto: McClelland and Stewart, pp. 80-92.
Weber, Max.
1958. *The City*. Glencoe: Free Pr.
Wellman, Barry, Steve Gates, Barry Craven and Marilyn Whitaker.
1970. "Community Ties and Support Systems." Toronto: Centre for Urban and Community Studies, University of Toronto, Working Paper No. 2.
Wellman, Barry.
1974. "The Form and Function of Future Communities." In L.S. Bourne, R.D. MacKinnon, J. Siegel, and J.W. Simmons, *Urban Futures for Central Canada: Perspectives on Forecasting Urban Growth and Form*. Toronto: U of Toronto Pr, pp. 301-313.
Wellman, Barry and Barry Leighton.
1979. "Networks, Neighborhoods and Communities: Approaches to the Study of the Community Question." *Urban Affairs Quarterly* 14:363-400.
Whitaker, G.P.
1980. "Coproduction: Citizen Participation in Service Delivery." *Public Administration Review*, 40:240-246.
White, Morton and Lucia.
1962. *The Intellectual Versus the City*. New York: Mentor.
Whyte, William H.
1956. *The Organization Man*. Garden City, New York: Anchor.
Wirth, Louis.
1938. "Urbanism as a Way of Life." *American Journal of Sociology* 44:1-24.
Zeisel, John.
1973. "Symbolic Meaning of Space and the Physical Dimension of Social Relations." In Walton, J. and D.E. Carns, *Cities in Change: Studies on the Urban Condition*. Boston: Allyn, pp. 262-263.

Glossary

back-to-the-city movement - the revived attraction of the inner city to young couples as a place to live and raise children

census - an inventory of defined populations within specified areas at particular moments in time

citizen power - the allocation of power to make decisions to citizens affected by these decisions

city planning - the profession of setting environmental goals and developing design guidelines for cities

co-production - the involvement of citizens in reducing the costs of service delivery through direct voluntary assistance or adjustment of expectations to meet service levels

congruence - the matching of individual values with the surrounding environment

council-board of control - a form of urban government where there is a general council and an elected board of control which forms an executive committee

council-commission - a form of urban government where there is an elected council and mayor and a council-appointed board of commissioners responsible for the administration of the city

council-committee - a form of urban government where municipal councillors are appointed to standing committees responsible for such things as parks and recreation, traffic and parking, public works, and safety

council-manager - a form of urban government where council forms policy and an appointed manager is in charge of administration

defensible space - the design of physical environment in a way that it provides greater opportunities to reduce crime

disgovernance - the syndrome whereby cities have become unable to provide adequate levels of services or to respond to urban decline

172

ethnic villagers - a grouping of people belonging to one ethnic group living in an inner-city area surrounded by institutions (e.g., churches and stores) which cater to their religion and traditions

filtering - the passing down of aging housing stock from high to low income groups

gatekeeper - individuals within municipal government who develop and manage administrative rules for allocating scarce resources

gentrification - the upgrading of old inner-city housing stock

human ecology - a theoretical perspective which sets out to explain changes in urban social structure based on competition for scarce land and resources

horizontal community - a community where the control of important community functions lies in the hands of local people

ladder of citizen participation - a conceptual scheme which classifies different levels of citizen power

latent demand - a demand for services that evolves when consumers discover they need them and that others have them

liberated community - the aspatial, primary social network that people maintain with family and friends

metropolitan government - usually a two-tier level of government where independent cities share responsibilities for region-wide service delivery (e.g., police, fire and transit)

myth of suburbia - description of suburbs as places of intense interaction between people with similar backgrounds

physical determinism - a point of view which argues that an improvement in physical surroundings should lead to an improvement in social behaviour

political economy - a theoretical approach which emphasizes a structural explanation of urban change focussing on economic institutions affecting individual behaviour

population turnaround - movement of urban people to rural areas

potential demand - future demand for services based on growth in population groups needing these services

primary group - a social group in which close personal relations develop through face-to-face interaction

redevelopment - a renewal scheme which involves purchasing properties, demolishing all existing buildings, and rebuilding according to new plans

rehabilitation - a renewal scheme which involves upgrading existing structures through an injection of capital and resources

sample survey - a study in which information is gathered from a fraction of the population

saved community - the local support that people derive from neighbours and friends in close proximity to them *social area analysis* - an ecological technique developed to use census information in describing urban areas according to social rank, family status, and ethnicity

social impact assessment - an evaluation of the total community response to changes coming about as a result of large-scale development

social indicators - a compilation of statistics used as measures of the state of urban living

social networks - social ties (both primary and secondary) which develop between people and others with whom they come into regular contact

social power perspective - a theoretical perspective which examines the interaction of groups in terms of their ability to influence the allocation of resources

spillover - the growth of urban structures and functions beyond city boundaries

tax revolt movement - a grass-roots political response to increased property tax assessment

urbanism - the ways of living in cities

urbanization - the growth of cities due to reclassification of rural areas to urban, the excess of city dwellers through natural increase over rural dwellers, and the movement of rural people to cities

urban reform - a movement towards redefining city boundaries to include surrounding areas so as to improve the city's revenue sources

urban renewal - the policy of investing in the upgrading of older inner-city areas

urban service goals - determining the efficiency, effectiveness, responsiveness, and equity of urban service allocations

vertical community - a community where the control of important functions lie outside of the community

zoning by-law - a legal restriction on the type of development allowed in different parts of the city

Name Index

Subject Index